PLAY-OF-COLOR QUILTING

24 Designs to Inspire Freehand Color Play

Bernadette Mayr *in collaboration with Irmgard Stängl and Gundula Manson*

Schiffer Publishing Ltd

4880 Lower Valley Road • Atglen, PA 19310

Originally published as *Farbenspiele* by Christophorus Verlag © 2015 Christophorus Verlag GmbH & Co. KG, Freiburg
Translated from the German by Omicron Language Solutions, LLC

Library of Congress Control Number: 2017955735

Type set in Frutiger LT Std/Minion Pro
ISBN: 978-0-7643-5533-2
Printed in China

Published by Schiffer Publishing, Ltd.
4880 Lower Valley Road
Atglen, PA 19310
Phone: (610) 593-1777; Fax: (610) 593-2002
E-mail: Info@schifferbooks.com
Web: www.schifferbooks.com

For our complete selection of fine books on this and related subjects, please visit our website at www.schifferbooks.com. You may also write for a free catalog.

Schiffer Publishing's titles are available at special discounts for bulk purchases for sales promotions or premiums. Special editions, including personalized covers, corporate imprints, and excerpts, can be created in large quantities for special needs. For more information, contact the publisher.

We are always looking for people to write books on new and related subjects. If you have an idea for a book, please contact us at proposals@schifferbooks.com.

Contents

Squares, Rectangles, Triangles

Log Cabin Pattern

Reverse Applique Technique and Open Edges

Foreword

This book is dedicated to colors. Here you will find large and small projects for very colorful, playful, wild, and geometric quilts. My approach is the freehand cutting technique I learned from quilt artist Nancy Crow. My trademarks are bright colors and black-and-white accents. I prefer to use commercial fabrics because I find the task of working with existing colors and patterns tantalizing. When designing a quilt, what matters to me most is the variety of colors, so it is only logical that in my workshop I sort fabrics according to color.

I keep my fabric stash in clear containers (the big ones with small wheels available at home improvement stores). The containers are clear so I can see the fabrics—and so they invite me to work with them. What a pool of ideas! I have a box with fabrics in shades of yellow/brown, black/gray, and purple/red/orange. I have two boxes each of blue and white color groups. Fabrics have the remarkable feature of regenerating while you are not looking, then they press against the lid from beneath and want to be worked with. From time to time, I put larger pieces neatly together and sort out unsuitable fabrics, after which I am again aware of the fabrics that I have and where they are. A box labeled "Started" sits a bit to the side.

Older generations of quilters have amassed considerable amounts of linens to make trousseaus, so for years I have been working with my Aunt Margret's bed linen, because white and natural white are good basic background colors. White linens, when overdyed, make beautiful quilt backings. But be selective; in a hurry once, I immediately regretted using a favorite duvet cover as a backing. I have not been able to find anything like it since.

I have often used pieces of fabric from sample books to sew into quilts (you will find some examples in this book). With the freehand cutting technique, you can also use packs of sewn-together squares or rolled-up strips in a totally unconventional way. Meanwhile, my denim collection has now shrunk from four containers to one.

And then there are those striped fabrics in every color that show up in many quilts, because what works better with bold colors than a black-and-white accent?

Wishing you a lot of fun sewing,
Bernadette Mayr

Who would have thought that cutting up and sewing together fabrics would provide so much enjoyment over the years? We work hand-in-hand and have a lot of fun together, as befits a good team.

Irmgard Stängl and
Gundula Manson

Materials

Sewing Appliances

Work with a normal sewing machine, a cutting mat (at least 18" × 24" [50 × 60 cm]), a rotary cutter (1.75" [4.5 cm] diameter), and with the usual sewing accessories, such as needles, thread, pins, scissors, chalk wheel, etc. To mark fabrics, heat-soluble, water-soluble markers and chalks work well, and often a hard or soft pencil. In addition, having a large cloth where you can pin your interim results is helpful. Finally, a steam iron is a good idea for ironing. Use a sprayer, such as a flower sprayer, to dampen fabrics prior to ironing.

Rulers

A ruler is essential for measuring and cutting larger blocks to the same size, for even strips, for the border strips, and as an aid for cutting many identical strips and pieces of fabric, as well as for making the outer edges even. Have a long (6.5" × 24" [15 × 60 cm]) quilt ruler and a 7⅞" × 7⅞" (20 × 20 cm) square ruler at hand.

Amounts of Fabric

When buying fabric without having a specific project in mind, I recommend buying one "long quarter" per color (a long quarter is 44" wide [112 cm] and 10" [25 cm] long and cut crosswise from the bolt, from selvedge to selvedge). A "fat quarter" (fat quarter = 22" wide and 20" long [50 × 55 cm]) results when a half meter of fabric is divided once along the fold.

There are amounts of fabric available for quilts in the event that you go fabric shopping especially for these. Remember that when you work freehand, you often need more fabric than when using traditional techniques, since you have to keep cutting off overlapping edges, cut large pieces into smaller ones, or fill in holes with fabric.

Fleece

All the quilts, wall quilts, and cushions described here are padded with medium-thick polyester fleece. You can also use other fleeces you are familiar with. Cotton fleece is flatter and heavier than polyester fleece but is preferred by many quilters because of its natural fiber.

Thread

Sew colorful fabrics with neutral-colored thread, such as gray, beige, or brown. In black-and-white quilts, the thread color should also be black or white. The quilting thread should match the color of the fabric. When you sew an applique, the thread must match the color of the fabric on top when it is stitched down.

Techniques

Freehand Cutting

When cutting freehand, you work without using a ruler and stencil. Use the grid lines of the cutting mat as a guide and rely on your sense of proportion. Use the piece you cut first as your pattern for size and shape. It is normal that the pieces and seams shift when material is pieced together. Cut away the extra fabric parts, or add them to small pieces by sewing on another piece of fabric. You will soon be able to assess how much fabric is lost in the seam allowances.

When cutting out a larger number of strips or squares, place the ruler on the desired inch mark, but be generous. You do not need to measure that accurately, because a quarter inch or so does not matter.

For most projects, plan to make all the blocks the same size. In this case, use a ruler and cut out exactly.

Ironing

With fabrics that are cut and sewn freehand, you may pull, tug, and dampen them and also move the iron back and forth vigorously. Do not worry that a block will get out of shape, because you will eventually trim it to shape anyway.

Use a steam iron or get a spray bottle to dampen the fabric. First iron the dampened fabric on the wrong side to smooth the seam allowances flat, then again on the right side to iron the seams completely open. Pull the fabric edges slightly away from the iron so that you do not iron in any wrinkles. Iron the seam allowances together to one side, not apart.

When you sew the blocks of the quilt top together, follow the rules for laying the seam allowances in Lesson 9, "Piecing the Quilt Together Efficiently." Also dampen these seams and place the iron on the seams on the wrong side of the fabric, so that the seam allowances are laid in the right direction. After that, also iron from the correct side. Press the seam allowances of the border strips outward.

Quilting

I quilted the quilts in this book with my longarm quilting machine. The suggested quilt patterns also work, in part, for hand quilting and quilting with a normal sewing machine. Choose for yourself.

Fabrics

Fabrics with a range of color from light to dark offer a broad palette of all the shades of one color. If you buy a quarter yard (quarter meter) of every color combination, you have a good selection.

There are rainbow fabrics with bright colors and subtle transitions of color. You can find these fabrics in quilt shops. Some dyers can produce extremely fine color gradients. Cut out the color groups you want from these fabrics. If some colors are repeated, it does not matter.

There are very usable packs of fabric available for sale that are already sorted and cut out, or they can be ordered in quilt shops. Select solid-color fabrics such as Amish packs or fabrics with light patterns, which seen from a distance appear like solid-color fabrics (so-called false solids). Here also there can be several pieces of the same color. For some of the suggested quilts, the 2.5"-wide (6.5 cm) strips that are available rolled up as "candy," "lollipops," or "jelly rolls" work well.

Working with Sample Books

I like to use sample books and fabric swatches from decorator or interior design stores. Anything bigger in size than 2" × 2" (5 × 5 cm) is welcome. But I use only cotton; other materials are at most suitable for wall quilts. Warning: since you cannot prewash fabrics from sample books, there is a big risk they will become discolored!

Many fabric samples are sorted by color and fastened to a backing. As a rule, you can easily tear off or cut away these pieces. In some sample books you just have to loosen a screw, which is the most practical. Often the books are riveted. Plastic rivets can be opened by force; use a strong screwdriver as a lever. Metal rivets usually put up fierce resistance. In this case, the fabric pieces will have to be individually cut out with scissors.

Even removing the labels on swatches will take some work. While many labels can be removed by briefly ironing over them, some of the adhesive always remains, which can later penetrate through the right side of the fabric in an unattractive way. Therefore, cut off all labels and paper backing with scissors. This is tedious, but it is worth the effort. Sit in your most comfortable chair with a big wastepaper basket next to you and enjoy a great movie at the same time.

Sometimes these sample cloth pieces will not get you very far. Come to terms with the amount that you have, or surround the central part with an interesting border to enlarge the quilt.

Color Distribution

Borders

There are ways to apportion the quilt top areas that I particularly love. For example, I like to work an interesting and contrasting cross stripe into the upper portion of a quilt. When the cover lies on the bed, the stripe lies exactly on the fold for the pillows and thus creates a good effect. A border of this kind works well as a vertical central stripe or at the foot of a bed (pattern: Strange Birds).

Scattering

If you distribute colors over the quilt top, you should make sure that they look as if they have been scattered at random (which they are not, of course). Do not put two identical colors next to each other, and distribute the light and dark colors evenly. Pay attention to very striking colors or fabrics and place them far apart (patterns: Shadow Boxes, Red Flowers, and Diver's Paradise).

Grouping

Sometimes it makes sense to group some colors into a four-patch block or into rows. Distribute these groups over different places on the quilt top (patterns: Star Block Blues, Swirl, Denim Blossoms, and M-star).

Sorting

To make sure your arrangement of uniform blocks does not get boring, you can sort them by color. Sort either from light (above) to dark (below), or with bright fabrics in the middle and dark on the outside (and vice versa). Or group the colors by red, blue, green, yellow, and so on (patterns: Swirl, Stand-Up Chopsticks, Jeans plus Jeans, and Colored Saucers).

Colors

For us patchworkers, the color of a fabric has a special significance because, unlike painters, who can mix their palette, quilters have to work with the colors they are given. This is the reason we need so many fabrics.

For example, we need cornflower blue, royal blue, midnight blue, denim blue, delft blue, cerulean blue, blue-green, sky blue, gray blue, indigo blue, cobalt blue, ultramarine blue, pale blue . . . and all of them in solid color, flecked, striped, plaid, floral, swirled, spotted, and marbled. The result is a well-filled fabric cabinet. The selection of colors for a quilt is a matter of feeling and taste. The quilt should fit into the environment and, above all, please you. I personally prefer bright colors and add black-and-white accents. Here you will also find pastel colors and quilts with only two or three colors. Decide for yourself. What is important: do not use fabrics or colors you do not like!

Red — *for fiery, powerful quilts. All the red tones (from pink to orange to fire engine red) can be combined. If the quilt is to radiate warmth, yellow and purple do this well. Turquoise and bright green make cool accents.*

Yellow — *yellow tones warm the heart and bring sunshine into every room. When combined with light green, spring is already here. Van Gogh often used yellow together with its complementary color, blue, to convey the impression of space and lightness.*

Blue — *is for sky, ice, and water spaces that we associate with cold and cooling. Could a blue quilt cool us off on hot summer nights? It would be worth an experiment. You can combine yellow and orange with blue.*

Brown — *the color of the Earth. Natural materials such as wood and leather make a room comfortable. Brown, in earlier times looked down on as a "poor person's" color, is now considered the color of life's comforts. Just think about chocolate, coffee, and freshly baked bread*

Pastels — *these include all mild colors, as if you diluted the colors of your paintbox with white. Pastel tones lend rooms elegance and lightness. You can combine all pastel colors with each other and arrange them against a light background.*

Green — *the color of nature and growth. There are warm and cold green tones. In green quilts, a small portion of red always works powerfully and well.*

Multicolored — *as soon as you use all the colors of the rainbow you get a distinctive, unique piece. Black-white accents in the form of fabric strips are almost a "must."*

Denim — *the indigo of blue jeans is one of the magic colors that matches with all the other ones. Here you cannot go wrong. Both very bold colors and black and white create a beautiful effect.*

SQUARES, RECTANGLES, TRIANGLES

Lesson 1:
Basic Shapes

Strips

Lay the folded fabric on your cutting mat with the bigger piece of cloth lying on the table. Set a folded edge of the fabric on a grid line of the mat to keep it at a right angle. Cut the fabric from selvedge to selvedge, in strips as wide as the side length of the planned squares/rectangles/strips. You can cut several layers of fabric at the same time. Hold the fabric tight on the cutting mat with your fingertips. Be careful when using a rotary cutter: you could injure yourself because a ruler edge does not offer any protection (keep Band-Aids handy). Cut quickly through the fabric by eye; a millimeter or so does not matter. If your cutting line goes a bit askew, that is irrelevant.

Squares/Rectangles

Lay the squares/rectangles on the cutting mat individually, or up to four fabric strips one atop the other. First, if necessary, cut away the selvedges. Align the right edge or the left edge (depending on whether you are right- or left-handed) along one of the grid lines. Use the next marking as a guide, according to the desired edge length of the fabric piece. Set the roller cutter on the bottom edge of the fabric and cut through all layers of fabric upward without using a ruler. It does not matter if your cutting line goes a bit askew.

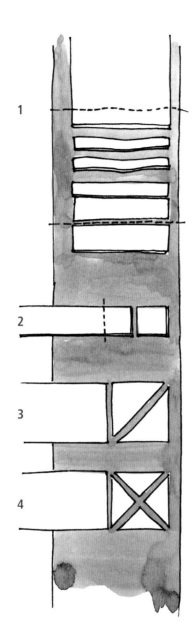

1

2

3

4

1. Lay the folded fabric on the cutting mat. Cut strips of the desired width. The grid lines of the cutting mat serve as a guide. Either cut strips freehand or use a ruler, but without measuring to the exact millimeter.

2. Cut the squares or rectangles in the desired width from the strips. Run a rotary cutter vertically from the bottom upward. Use the grid lines of the cutting mat as a guide.

3. A square divided once for two triangles, where the straight grain lies along the short sides.

4. Square divided twice for four triangles, where the straight grain lies along the long sides.

Triangles

Cut fabric into a square of the size indicated and divide it once on the bias into two triangles, or divide larger squares on the bias twice into four triangles. Cut without using a ruler.

TIP
If you have to cut a lot of squares, rectangles, or triangles for a large quilt, use a ruler to help. This way you avoid accidentally cutting the pieces so that they are either always bigger or smaller and thus do not unnecessarily use too much fabric. Use the ruler only as a straightedge for the rotary cutter. You do not have to measure accurately.

Lesson 2:
Double Cutting
Projects: Swirl, Evening Bag, and Fire

I understand double cutting as cutting through two layers of fabric at the same time. It is important that both pieces of fabric are right side up. As soon as you switch the colors, and thus put the pieces back in their previous position, the seams on the edges will match exactly. This makes two blocks in which the colors are inverted.

Step 1: Lay two cutout fabric pieces on the cutting mat, both with the right side up.

Step 2: Use the roller cutter to cut through both layers at the same time. (To find how many cuts to make, and which cuts these are, please refer to the instructions for each project.)

Step 3: Now switch the fabric pieces without twisting them around. You get two blocks whose colors are diametrically opposite.

Step 4: Now you can sew. Start with the short seams, then join the long ones.

Step 5: Iron the block and cut it exactly to the desired size.

Pattern "Swirl"

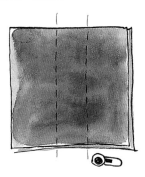

Lay two squares of different colors one atop the other. Both should be right side up. Cut through both layers twice lengthwise. Pull the pieces somewhat apart.

First sew the short seams. Press or iron the seam allowances to the outside.

Divide the two oblong fabric pieces again twice crosswise, again through both layers at the same time.

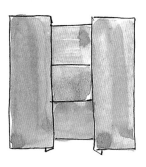

Join the long seams. Iron the seam allowance to the outside.

Switch the colors without twisting the pieces around. You get two blocks with a contrasting color combination.

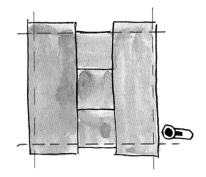

Finally, trim the block to the desired size.

Double Cutting

Pattern "Fire": Nine Patch Blocks

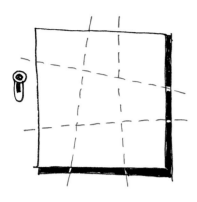

Lay two squares of different colors one atop the other. Both should be right side up. Make two slightly on-the-bias cuts through both layers, lengthwise and crosswise.

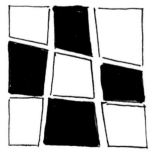

Switch the colors without twisting the pieces around. You get two blocks with a contrasting color combination.

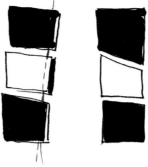

Lay the middle parts over the left ones and sew along the right edge. Sew from top to bottom and do not cut away the threads between the parts.

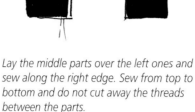

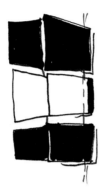

Unfold the sewn parts and lay the right ones over the middle parts. Sew the right edge again from the very top to the bottom. Do not cut away the threads between the parts.

Finally, join the crosswise seams. Press the seam allowances in opposite directions. Trim the finished nine-patch block to the desired size.

Pattern "Fire": Piecing Strips Together

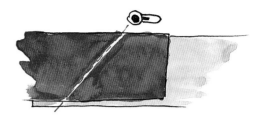

Overlap the ends of two strips that are next to each other, both with right side up.

Cut on the bias through both layers of fabric. Remove both the top and bottom short ends of the strips.

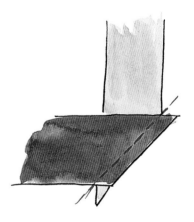

Join the bias seam and leave the protruding tips of the seam allowances. Unfold the strips, check that the shape is straight, and correct it if necessary. Trim away the protruding tips of the seam allowances.

Double Cutting

Lesson 3:
Attaching Triangles
Projects: Star Block Blues and Starry Sky

Such triangles are also called "connector corners." The starting shape is the corner of a rectangle or a square. If you want to attach a triangle, first cut off the corner of the basic shape. This gives you an idea of how big the added triangle should be.

Then cut out the triangle in the desired color. Add two seam allowance widths to the size of the cut triangle on the long edge, about ¾" (2 cm). If you have a lot of triangles to cut out, each time you should diagonally divide squares or rectangles that are big enough.

Now sew on the new triangle with its long edge to the basic shape. Iron the triangle to the outside and cut the shape again, because it will have shifted somewhat.

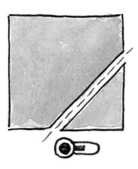

Cut off a corner from one square.

Attach a triangle (original size same as the square, folded on the bias once) to the resulting edge.

Fold the triangle outward. Press the seam with a fingernail.

Cut off the adjacent corner of the square on the bias.

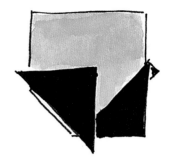

Sew on the second triangle.

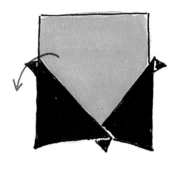

Fold the second triangle outward.

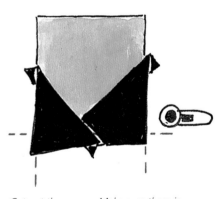

Cut out the square. Make sure there is enough space for the seam allowances of the added triangles.

Striped Quilt
7.45' × 5.91' (227 × 180 cm)

The sashing strips are inserted for two reasons: first, if the blocks of strips were pieced directly to each other, the effect would have been too lively; and second, the fabric strips were rather stiff, and this makes it extremely difficult to sew eight seams that all meet each other on our sewing machine. There is not much space here to use the freehand cutting technique; it is better to be careful and use a ruler for cutting.

▓ Materials
Fabric
- thirty-two different-striped fabrics (sample book), minimum size 13¾" × 13¾" (35 × 35 cm).
- ¼ yard (0.20 m) black for cornerstones.
- 2.18 yards (2.00 m) white for the sashings and the border.
- ⅞ yard (0.70 m) blue and white wide striped fabric, stripe width about 1⅝" (4 cm), for the binding.

Or a striped fabric of your choice:
a) 3.83 yards (3.50 m) each of lighter and darker striped fabric, strip width about 1³⁄₁₆" (3 cm).
b) 13.78" (0.35 m) each of eight different striped fabrics—light and dark—for four similar squares of each 13¾" × 13¾" (35 × 35 cm).

Other
- 8.2' × 6.56' (250 × 200 cm) backing fabric
- 8.2' × 6.56' (250 × 200 cm) volume fleece
- White quilting thread

▓ Instructions
Cutting Out
Cut the striped fabric into squares of exactly 13¾" × 13¾" (35 × 35 cm). Put together a matching pair, each time from a lighter and a darker fabric, in which one color appears twice; for example, blue-white (light) with blue-green (dark), or yellow-pink with yellow-black. Place the squares one atop the other, both right side up and with the stripes running parallel. First divide the squares twice diagonally into four triangles, then divide each triangle again from the tip to the long edge.

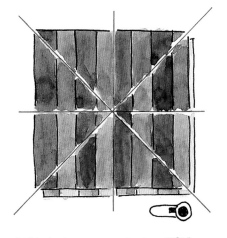

Divide the large squares (such as 13¾" × 13¾" [35 × 35 cm]) in the middle lengthwise and crosswise, then cut through them twice on the bias.

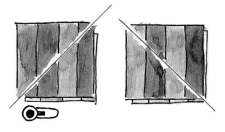

Cut through smaller squares (such as 7" × 7" [18 × 18 cm]) on the bias. One diagonally from left to right, one diagonally from right to left.

Thirty A blocks: Lay two light and two dark triangles opposite one another. The stripes of the upper and lower triangle run from bottom right to top left.

Thirty B blocks: Lay two light and two dark triangles opposite one another. The stripes of the upper and lower triangle run from bottom left to top right.

Sample Block B: Attach sashings with cornerstones. The length of the sashing matches the block edge; the cornerstone is as big as the width of the strip.

Piece the triangles together into four blocks, each of which has two of the same pattern (A blocks and B blocks). The long sides form the outer edge of the block. Sew the triangles together into a block.

Thirty A blocks
Each time, lay two light and two dark triangles opposite each other. The stripes of the upper and lower triangle run from bottom right to top left.

Thirty B blocks
Each time, lay two light and two dark triangles opposite each other. The stripes of the upper and lower triangle run from bottom left to top right.

Iron carefully, since all the outer edges are on the bias to the grain. Then cut out thirty blocks, each of the exact same size ($8^{17}/_{64}$" × $8^{17}/_{64}$" [21 × 21 cm]).

Sashings with Cornerstoness
Forty-eight cornerstones, black, exactly $1^{31}/_{32}$" × $1^{31}/_{32}$" (5 × 5 cm). Fifty-four sashings, exactly $1^{31}/_{32}$" × $8^{17}/_{64}$" (5 × 21 cm) (the length matches the block edge length).

Piecing Together the Center Section
Arrange the blocks into nine horizontal rows of seven blocks each. Start at the top left with a B block. Switch between the A and B blocks. Place them so that each time, a light edge is set next to the dark one of the next block. Distribute the colors harmoniously over the entire area. Piece together the blocks, the sashings, and the black cornerstones as described in Lesson 9. Iron the seam allowances to the sashings.

Four Striped Cornerstones in the Sashing Borders
Use four similar blocks (A or B) for the cornerstones in the sashing borders. Here they are exactly $5^{29}/_{32}$" × $5^{29}/_{32}$" (15 × 15 cm) in size. The $5^{29}/_{32}$" (15 cm) matches the width of the sashing border.

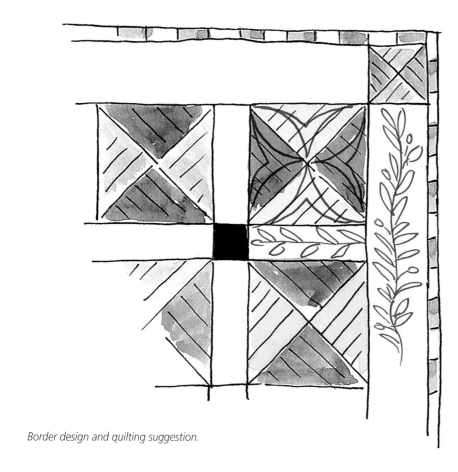

Border design and quilting suggestion.

Borders
(Lesson 10)
White, 5²⁹⁄₃₂" (15 cm) cutting width,
Four striped cornerstones, 5²⁹⁄₃₂" ×
5²⁹⁄₃₂" (15 × 15 cm)
(see above).

Quilting
(Lessons 11 and 12)
Assemble the backing, volume fleece, and quilt top one atop the other. Work with white quilting thread. With stripes such as this, I always think of awnings and sun loungers in the sunny South. Therefore, I chose a motif of olive branches for the borders and sashings. The striped blocks are quilted in an orange peel pattern with echo lines. If you quilt by hand, quilt just one border pattern on the white sashings and the border.

Binding
(Lesson 13)
Bind the basted edge with blue-white, wide-striped fabric strip, cutting width 2²³⁄₆₄" (6 cm), cut straight.

Quilt: Branches on the sashings.

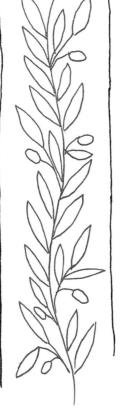

Quilt: Olive branches with olives on the sashing borders.

Quilt: Orange peel with echo on the blocks.

Swirl
6.23' × 5.58' (190 × 170 cm)

This quilt is a tribute to my friend, who allowed me to practice complementary colors with the swirl motif for hours using her watercolors. Working with silk has its own challenges, since silk pills a great deal, but its luster is unsurpassed.

▥ Materials
Fabric
- ⅓ yard (0.25 m) each of Honan silk fabrics in sixty-eight to seventy different colors, solid and textured.

Or as desired
- The same amount of cotton fabrics, solid, color gradients—all colors.

Other
- About 11 yards (10 m) very thin iron-on interfacing.
- 1 roll baking paper.
- 6.89' × 6.23' (210 × 190 cm) backing fabric.
- 6.89' × 6.23' (210 × 190 cm) volume fleece.
- Quilting thread in different colors.
- 25' (740 cm) anthracite-color satin bias binding.

▥ Instructions
Preparing the Color Combinations
Pin together two fabrics each time with matching colors. Combine the complementary colors red/green, purple/yellow, blue/orange. Vary them and find exciting color pairs. For example, combine red, rose, and pink with light, medium, and dark green; yellow, ocher, and brass with purple, blue, and turquoise; or light green and turquoise with brown tones. Do not match any complementary colors; choose a strong light-dark contrast, such as light gray or light blue with dark blue.

Combination blue/orange.

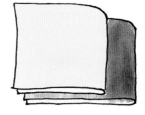
Combination yellow/purple.

Combination turquoise/brown.

  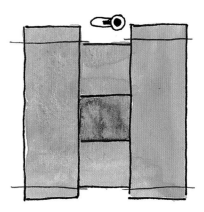

Put two squares (about 4¾" × 4¾" [12 × 12 cm]) one atop the other, both right side up. Make two straight lengthwise cuts, pull the pieces apart, and make two crosswise cuts in the middle section. Switch the colors, such as turquoise with a brown middle piece or brown with a turquoise middle piece.

Join the seams and cut back the protruding ends.

About 900 Squares in Complementary Contrasting Colors

(Lesson 1: Basic Shapes, Lesson 2: Double Cutting)

From each of the fabric pairs, cut out eight squares each of about 4²³⁄₃₂" × 4²³⁄₃₂" (12 × 12 cm) per ⅓ yard (0.25 m) of fabric. Lay two matching color squares one atop the other, both right side up (with silk there is usually no difference). First make two lengthwise cuts, each about 1³⁷⁄₆₄" (4 cm) away from the side edges. Pull apart the pieces. Then make two crosswise cuts in the middle length, again about 1³⁷⁄₆₄" (4 cm) from the top and bottom edges. Switch the colors, so that each time you make two different blocks. First sew the short cross seams, then the lengthwise seams. Cut off the protruding ends. Iron all seam allowances outward with a dry iron.

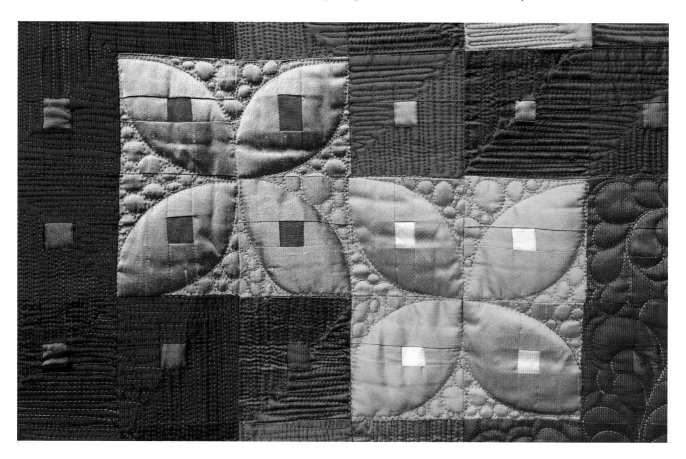

Place the iron-on interfacing on the ironing board with the adhesive side up. Arrange the sewn squares, wrong side down, close together on the ironing board. Spread baking paper on top and iron over with a hot iron. With this step, you line the back of the squares with a fine fleece, so that the edges of the silk fabric will not fray any more. You can use the baking paper several times.

Now cut out all the squares to the same size—here it is exactly $3\frac{5}{32}$" × $3\frac{5}{32}$" (8 × 8 cm). Pin the finished blocks one atop the other, according to color combination. This provides some order and later helps for arranging the colors. You need 868 blocks here but also need some extra ones for possible exchanges.

Design

Arrange the blocks on a design wall that is big enough. Here you are arranging thirty-one crosswise rows of twenty-eight squares each. Start in the center and arrange the successive color tones in a spiral shape rotating toward the right. When possible, create soft color transitions. Fill in the outer areas around the swirl with two rows running lengthwise, each in the same color, and interrupt it with different-colored four-patch blocks. Make sure that the long seams of the individual blocks run alternately lengthwise and crosswise. This gives an interesting effect, especially when you are using silk, since the fabrics gleam differently.

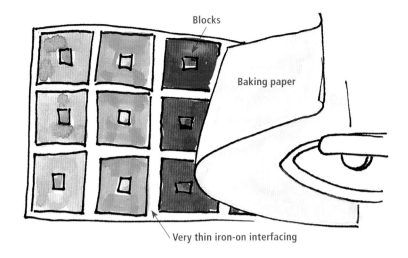

With silk fabric: Lay the blocks, wrong side down, on the adhesive side of some very thin iron-on interfacing. Spread baking paper on top and iron over with a hot iron. Cut all the blocks exactly (such as $3\frac{1}{4}$" × $3\frac{1}{4}$" [8 × 8 cm]).

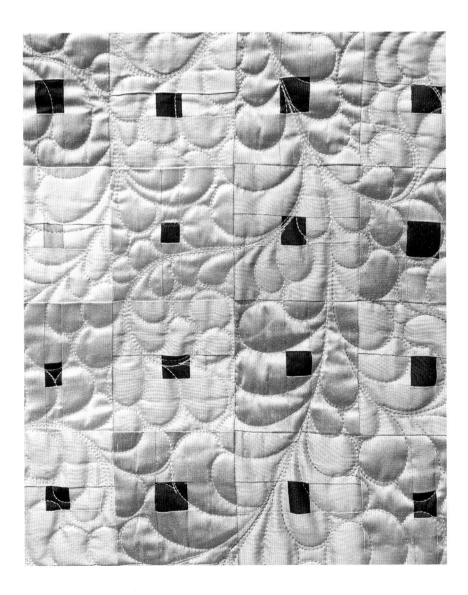

Piecing the Quilt Together

Sew the sections together as described in Lesson 9.

Quilting
(Lessons 11 and 12)

Assemble the backing, volume fleece, and quilt top one atop the other.

Use the longarm quilting machine to quilt a fine feather pattern on the swirl, dense length- and crosswise lines on the blocks around it, and four orange peels with a pebbled border on each of the four-patch blocks. You can quilt the meander pattern with the sewing machine or by hand on the swirl and orange peel on the background blocks.

Binding
(Lesson 13)

Bind the quilt edges with a prefolded, anthracite-colored satin bias binding.

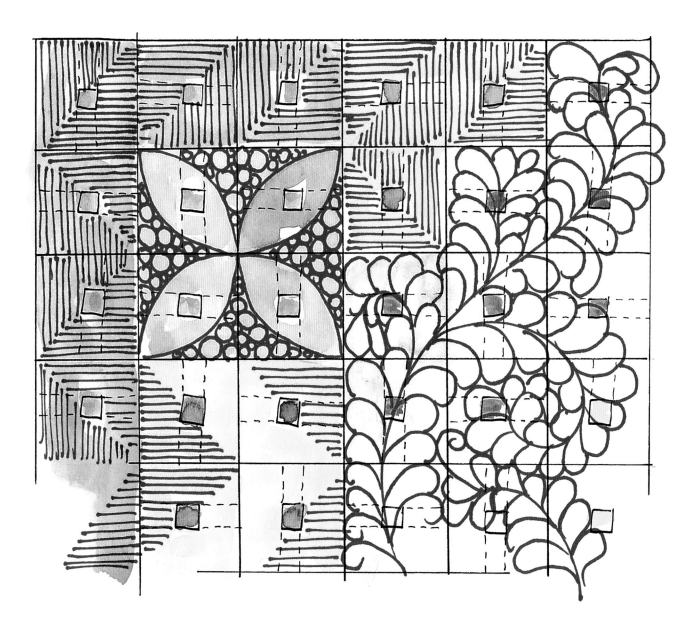

Arrangement of the blocks: the seams of the blocks run alternately lengthwise and crosswise. Quilting suggestion: cover the swirl with the feather pattern, the background with length- and crosswise stripes, and the four-patch blocks with orange peel and pebble background.

Fire
5.91' × 4.92' (180 × 150 cm)

In the Allgäu region of Germany on the Sunday after Ash Wednesday, people "drive out the winter" with huge beacons. This textile fire is created from crosswise stripes. Of course, I must include my black/white contrasts. What people will throw into a fire . . .

■ Materials
Fabric
- About 2¼ yards (2.00 m) in total of warm shades of yellow, orange, pink, and red to dark purple for the fire. Add eggplant, dark blue, and black/red patterned fabric for the surrounding area. Small amounts of pink and turquoise work well. Buy precut strips of 2⁹⁄₁₆" (6.5 cm) width; alternatively buy 5⅛" (0.13 m) per color and cut the strips yourself.
- About 2¼ yards (2.00 m) in total of various black tones, solid and lightly patterned, for the background (likewise precut or self-cut strips), and for the accent squares of 4²³⁄₃₂" × 4²³⁄₃₂" (12 × 12 cm).
- 4²³⁄₃₂" (0.12 m) white for the accents.

Other
- 7.22' × 5.91' (220 × 180 cm) backing fabric.
- 7.22' × 5.91' (220 × 180 cm) volume fleece.
- Fire-colored multicolor quilting thread.
- Anthracite-colored quilting thread.
- 7.5 yards (6.80 m) black satin bias strips for the binding.

■ Instructions
Preparation
Use a large design wall. A checkered or horizontally striped fabric covering is especially helpful. Work with precut and/or self-cut strips of precisely 2⁹⁄₁₆" (6.5 cm) width.

Twelve Black-white Nine Patch Blocks
(Lesson 1: Basic Shapes, Lesson 2: Double Cutting)

Cut six white and six black squares of about 4²¹⁄₆₄" × 4²¹⁄₆₄" (11 × 11 cm). Place one white and one black, one atop the other, both right side up. Cut through both layers at a time with two vertical and two horizontal cuts. Sort the colors into nine-patch blocks with a diametrically

Put one black and one white square (about 4⅓" × 4⅓" [11 × 11 cm]) one atop the other, both right side up. Cut through twice vertically and twice horizontally at a slight diagonal.

opposite color combination. Sew the blocks and cut them into squares of exactly 2⁹⁄₁₆" × 2⁹⁄₁₆" (6.5 × 6.5 cm) so you can conveniently work them into the fire stripes.

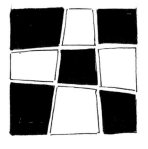

Switch the colors and sew the pieces together. Trim the nine-patch blocks to 2½" × 2½" (6.5 × 6.5 cm).

Composition

Put the fire-colored fabric strips crosswise on your cutting mat and cut pieces of different sizes at a bias angle. Change the cutting direction from lower left to upper right and from lower right to upper left. The strip piece can be between ⅛ yard (4 cm) and ⅓ yard (30 cm) long.

Now the issue is color distribution; work from the bottom up. Arrange strips of different lengths on the design wall. Keep to straight, horizontal rows. Start with the yellow and orange pieces and distribute them like flames on the design wall. Add the pink and the patterned purple pieces. Intersperse the black-and-white nine-patch blocks. Arrange red and dark-purple pieces beside the flames. Always end with black fabric at the right and left. Plan for individual flying sparks by marking the place with pins and little yellow snippets.

When you are finished, the pieces placed on the design wall should cover an area about 2⅝ yards (240 cm) high and 2⅞ yards (170 cm) wide. Now start to sew the rows together.

Piecing the Rows Together
(Lesson 2: Double Cutting)
Take two prepared strip pieces and place them crosswise on the cutting mat. Both should be right side up. Place them exactly horizontal and use the grid lines as a guide. Place the short bias edge of one strip so that it overlaps the end of the adjacent strip.

Cut along the bias edge of the top strip. This way, you cut the edges of both strips at the same bias angle. Now sew the two pieces together along this cut. When sewing, leave the tips protruding a seam allowance wide. Iron the seam allowances together to the darker or the softer fabric, and cut off the protruding tips of the seam allowances.

Place the strips before and after each seam along a grid line of the cutting mat to check whether you have made the row straight, and correct it if necessary.

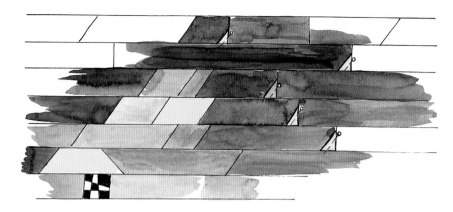

Arrange the fire-colored strips on the design wall, keeping to horizontal rows.

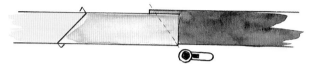

Both strips should be right side up. Place a bias end over the adjacent end and cut along the edge of the top strip, or make a bias cut through both pieces of fabric. Remove any unneeded small pieces.

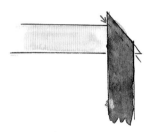

When sewing it all together, leave the tips of the seam allowances protruding. Unfold, iron, and cut off the tips.

TIP
Correct a false seam by gently pushing the fabric row straight and pressing the resulting fold toward the seam. Use your fingernail to firmly smooth out the new seam line, which then runs at an acute angle along the old seam. Sew from the wrong side along the crease. If all else fails, cut the seam away completely with the rotary cutter. Align the short edges again and correct the angle, then sew again. This way, you do not need to pull anything apart.

The "sparks" are made of yellow triangles, of which you will have plenty because of all the bias cuts. Place the triangles with the long edge to the left, pointing to the fire.

Sew the quilt until it is finished, row by row, and fill out the ends left and right with black pieces, until all the rows are the same width—here this is about 1¾ yards (160 cm). Sew thirty-eight rows. The top and bottom rows are pure black. You should also design the black rows using varied black and black-patterned fabrics.

Finally, sew all the rows together. If you shift the pattern of the colors when doing this, it does not matter. However, keep an eye on the nine-patch blocks and the sparks, so that they appear to be distributed randomly after the rows are pieced together. Sew the rows together, alternately from left to right and from right to left. This way, the top will hardly bunch up at all.

TIP

To check the length of the rows, you can make a mark on your work table with tape at 1¾ yards (160 cm) away from the table edge.

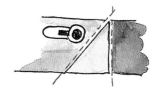

Insert the "sparks": Place a triangle right side up on the strip. Cut along the bias edge.

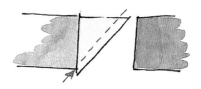

Sew the spark triangle to the black strips along the long edge.

Unfold the triangle. Cut off any protruding tips of the black strip.

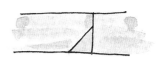

Then sew to the right edge of the adjacent black strip.

Quilting
(Lessons 11 and 12)

Assemble the backing, volume fleece, and quilt top one atop the other. Quilt irregular "Baptist Fan" patterns such as clouds of smoke on the black background and a flame pattern on the fire colors. With the longarm quilting machine, you can also decorate the fan curves densely with border patterns.

Binding
(Lesson 13)

Bind the basted edge with black bias binding.

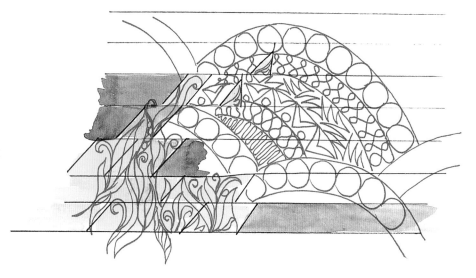

Quilting suggestion: flames on the fire colors, Baptist fans on the black areas.

Star Block Blues
2³⁄₈ × 2 yards (215 × 175 cm)

Have the courage to use black! The contrast here between the pastel colors and the black star points creates an exciting look. Freehand cut stars are nothing new, but it is so much fun to sew them. These are made out of precut strip packs, but they still look fresh and crazy.

■ Materials
Fabrics

- 5⁷⁄₈ yards (5.30 m) total amount: about eighty strips—2⁹⁄₁₆" (6.5 cm) wide each—of pastel colored batik fabrics for the background.
- 3 × ¹⁄₃ yard (0.25 m) each of yellow, blue, and orange (or remnants, total amount about ⁷⁄₈ yard [0.70 m])—solid or lightly patterned—for the star centers.
- 3 yards (2.70 m) black, solid, for the star points.
- ¼ yard (0.20 m) striped black and white, strip width of about ¹⁄₃" (1 cm), for the accent stripes for border 1.
- 1¹⁄₃ yards (1.20 m) light blue for border 2 and some star centers.

Other

- 2⁵⁄₈ × 2¼ yards (230 × 195 cm) backing fabric.
- 2⁵⁄₈ × 2¼ yards (230 × 195 cm) volume fleece.
- Lilac-colored quilting thread 26¼ ft. (8.00 m) lilac bias binding for the binding.

■ Instructions
Cutting Out

If you have not bought/found any precut batiks, cut your pastel batiks from selvedge in strips of 2⁹⁄₁₆" (6.5 cm) wide. Use a ruler, but you do not need to measure accurately to the millimeter. Divide the strips into squares of about 2⁹⁄₁₆" × 2⁹⁄₁₆" (6.5 × 6.5 cm). You can get sixteen squares per strip from selvedge to selvedge, which is enough for two stars.

For the black star points, cut out squares of 2⁹⁄₁₆" × 2⁹⁄₁₆" (6.5 × 6.5 cm) and divide each one along the bias.

Cut away one corner from a batik square (2½" × 2½" [6.5 × 6.5 cm]).

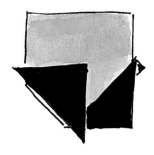

Sew on the second triangle.

You need per star:
- one center square of about 2⁹⁄₁₆" × 2⁹⁄₁₆" (6.5 × 6.5 cm).
- four black squares of about 2⁹⁄₁₆" × 2⁹⁄₁₆" (6.5 × 6.5 cm), each one cut on the bias for the star points.
- eight colored batik squares of about 2⁹⁄₁₆" × 2⁹⁄₁₆" (6.5 × 6.5 cm) for the background.

154 Star Blocks
(Lesson 1: Basic Shapes,
Lesson 3: Attaching Triangles)
Cut off one of the bottom corners on the bias from a batik square and attach a black triangle with its long side to the resulting edge. Fold the black corner outward and smooth out the seam with a fingernail, then cut off the adjacent corner. Sew on a diametrically opposite black triangle and fold it outward again. Sew on four such units, each time out of the same fabric. They will be especially irregular and interesting if you cut off corners of different sizes. Iron the units. Cut the units square by eye or use a ruler. Use the grid lines of your cutting mat as a guide.

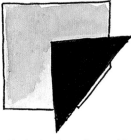

Attach a black triangle to the resulting edge (2½" × 2½" [6.5 × 6.5 cm], divided once along the bias).

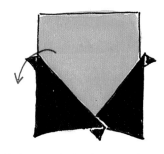

Fold the second triangle outward.

Fold the triangle outward. Press the seam with your fingernail.

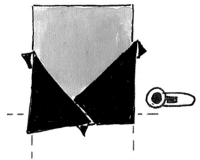

Cut out the square. Make sure there is enough space for the seam allowances of the sharp black points.

Cut the adjacent corner of the batik square on the bias.

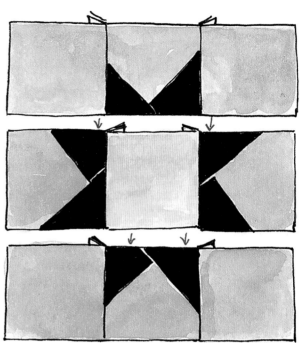

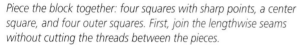

Piece the block together: four squares with sharp points, a center square, and four outer squares. First, join the lengthwise seams without cutting the threads between the pieces.

Then join the crosswise seams. Press the seam allowances in opposite directions.

Put each star block together individually. Piece together the four star point units, the four colored squares, and the blue center square into a star block. Work using the chain-piecing technique, without cutting the threads between the units. Press the seam allowance toward the plain squares each time.

Sew at least 154 star blocks. Press the seams of the two opposite star point units to the center and those of the others outward, or vice versa. Finally, cut all the star blocks to a common size. Keep in mind to cut so that there is sufficient seam allowance around the star points. Here, the cutting measurement is exactly 6" × 6" (15 × 15 cm) per block.

Cut out the blocks precisely (here, 6" × 6" [15 × 15 cm]).

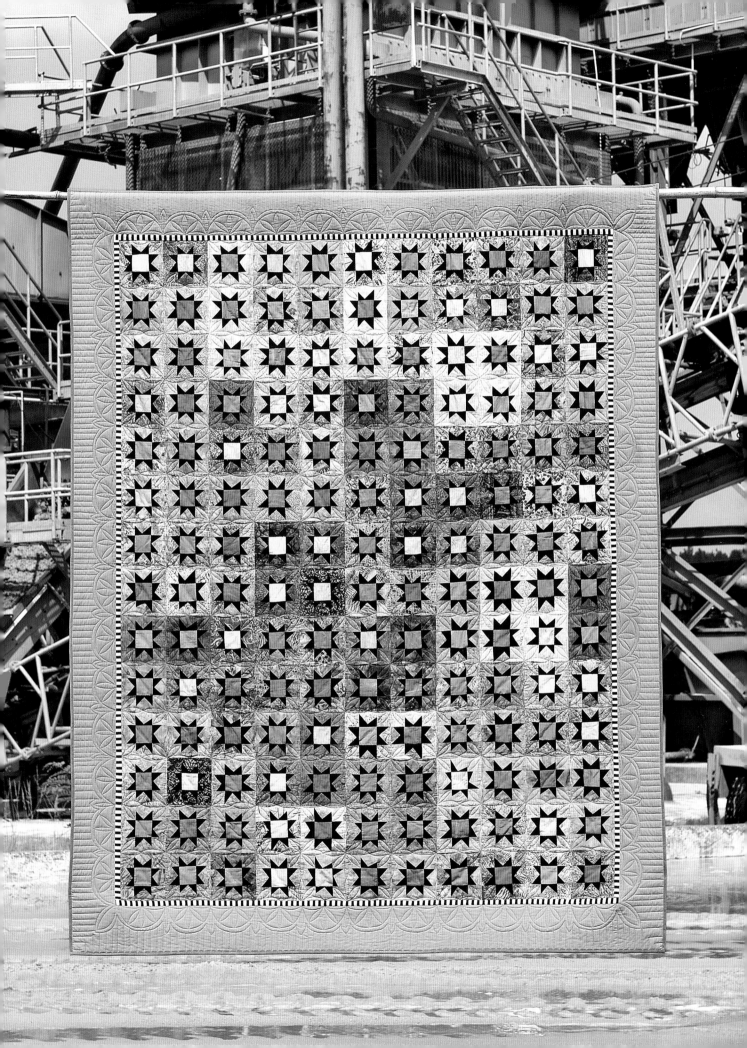

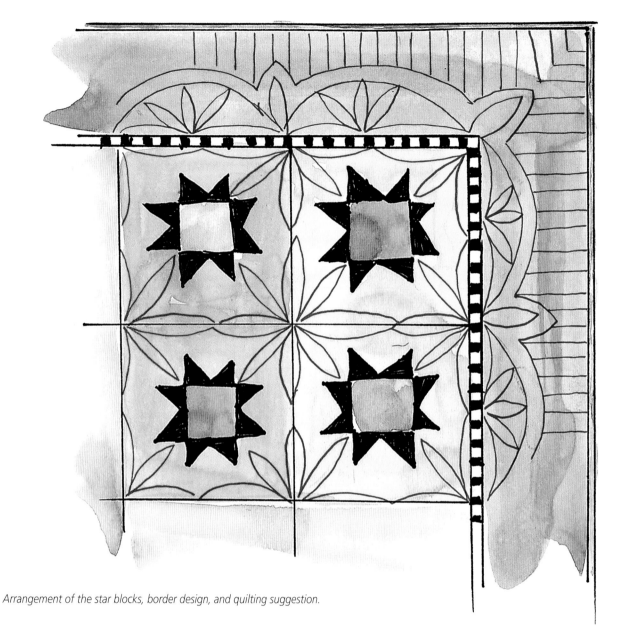

Arrangement of the star blocks, border design, and quilting suggestion.

Piecing the Quilt Together
(Lesson 9)

Arrange the blocks in fourteen horizontal rows of eleven blocks each. Make four-patch groups of similar colors and small rows. Distribute the striking colors so that they are farther apart from each other. Sew the blocks together as described in Lesson 9.

Borders
(Lesson 10)

First Border: black-and-white striped accent stripes, cutting width 1³⁄₁₆" (3 cm), straight corners.

Second Border: Medium blue solid, cutting width 6" (15 cm), straight corners.

Quilting
(Lessons 11 and 12)

Assemble the backing, volume fleece, and quilt top, one atop the other.

Quilt flowers with pointed leaves at the block intersections. Reflect the motif as an echo on the border or find another border pattern that you like.

Binding
(Lesson 13)

Bind the basted edge with a lilac bias binding.

Stand-Up Chopsticks
2⅝ yards × 2⅓ yards (235 × 210 cm)

Our eyes can be fooled easily; the colored chopsticks appear to be standing upright and casting a shadow on the quilt.

▥ Materials
Fabrics
- Sample book: ninety colors for 168 rectangles of about 3½" × 5⅛" (9 × 13 cm) (two chopsticks each are the same); separate out the natural-white fabric.
- 1 yard (0.90 m) dark gray for the shadows.
- 11 yards (10 m) muslin or natural white for the background.
- ⅔ yards (0.60 m) black and white striped—stripe width about ⅓" (1 cm)—for the binding.

Or alternatively for the chopsticks
- 1 yard (0.90 m) rainbow fabric.
- five ombre fabrics, light to dark: 6" (15 cm) each in red, yellow, blue, green, and brown.
- Fabric pack: about sixty assorted solid-color squares of about 4¾" × 4¾" (12 × 12 cm) (three chopsticks each are the same).

Other
- 2¾ yards × 2⅝ yards (250 × 230 cm) backing fabric.
- 2¾ yards × 2⅝ yards (250 × 230 cm) volume fleece.
- Natural white quilting thread.

> **TIP**
> If you like to sew exactly, you can also piece together and sew this block using the "sewing on paper" method.

▥ Instructions
Cutting Out
(Lesson 1: Basic Shapes)
For the chopsticks, cut out 168 rectangles of about 1½" × 5⅛" (4 × 13 cm). Several chopsticks can be of the same color.

For the shadows, cut out seven strips—4¾" (12 cm) wide—of dark gray from selvedge to selvedge. Cut out 168 squares of about 4" × 4" (10 × 10 cm) from the muslin for the areas above and below the shadows, and cut the rest of the fabric from selvedge to selvedge into 4"-wide (10 cm) strips. Use a ruler to cut them out, but you do not need to measure accurately to the millimeter.

168 Chopsticks Blocks

Sew one each of a 4¾"-wide (12 cm) dark gray and a 4"-wide (10 cm) muslin strip together along the long edge. Iron the seam to the gray fabric. Cut out a total of 168 units, each 1½" (4 cm) wide, for the shadows.

Place the units at a 45 degree angle on a cutting mat. Use a diagonal grid line as a guide. Cut off the lower-left corner of a gray-fabric shadow unit vertically. Divide a 4" × 4" (10 × 10 cm) square along the bias. Sew the shadow unit between the diagonals. Start sewing from the lower-left corner. The light fabric of the shadow unit protrudes from the right edge and can be cut off now or later.

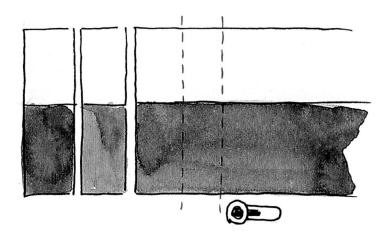

Sew together one strip of shadow fabric (4¾" [12 cm]) and background fabric (4" [10 cm]). Cut out units of 1⅕" (4 cm) wide.

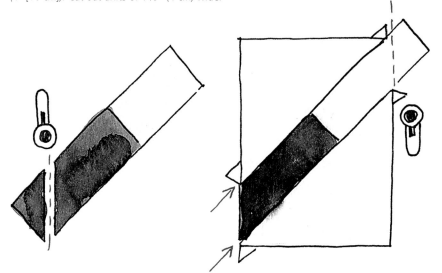

Cut out a rectangle to make a chopstick (1⅕" × 5⅛" [4 × 13 cm]).

Piecing together a shadow unit: cut off the lower-left corner of the shadow fabric.

Attach two muslin triangles to the sides of the shadow unit. Cut away any protruding fabric.

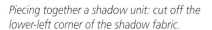

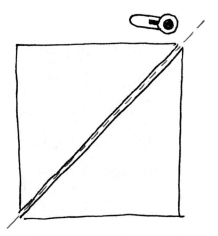

Divide a square (4" × 4" [10 × 10 cm]) along the bias.

Iron the seam allowance to the dark fabric. Now place the colored chopstick on the left edge of the unit. Iron the seam to the chopstick. Then attach a 4"-wide (10 cm) strip of muslin to the left chopstick edge as long as the chopstick. Again, iron the seam to the chopstick. Now cut the upper edge straight, by eye or using a ruler, and cut away the protruding right end of the shadow unit. Sew a 4"-wide (10 cm) strip on to the top edge of the block. Sew together a total of 168 such blocks.

Using a square ruler, cut all the blocks to a uniform size—here it is 7" × 7" (18 × 18 cm). Be sure that the first two cuts are lined up at the lower left corner of the chopstick. As little as possible should be cut away there.

Sewing Plan

Arrange the blocks on a design wall, with the lighter chopsticks at the top of the quilt and the darker ones at the bottom. Arrange the blocks in fourteen horizontal rows of twelve blocks each. Stagger the block arrangement. Fill in the gaps at the sides with strips of muslin about 4" (10 cm) wide, as long as the blocks.

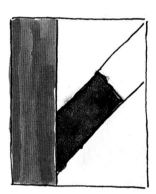

Attach colored chopsticks to the left edge.

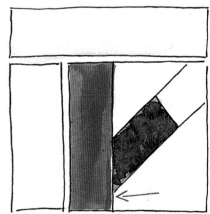

Sew on the background to the left edge of the chopstick (4" [10 cm]). Cut the top and right edges of the block so that they are even, and sew 4" (10 cm) of the background to the top edge. Trim all the blocks to the same size.

Piecing the Quilt Together

First sew the horizontal rows and piece these together, one below another, onto the quilt top. Attach a 4"-wide (10 cm) muslin strip, as long as the quilt edge, both to the bottom edge and right edge. If necessary, straighten the outer edges.

Quilting

(Lessons 11 and 12)

Assemble the backing, volume, and quilt top, one atop the other. **Longarm quilting:** Quilt using natural-colored thread, using a curving upright feather pattern in the in-between spaces; for example, start each time in the "V" between the chopstick and its shadow.

Suggestion for hand quilting: Quilt narrow upright rectangles in the seams and on the light surfaces, in a regular or irregular arrangement, the same size as the colored chopsticks.

Binding

(Lesson 13)

Bind the quilt edge with a black-and-white-striped, straight-cut, doubled strip of fabric, cutting width 2⅓" (6 cm).

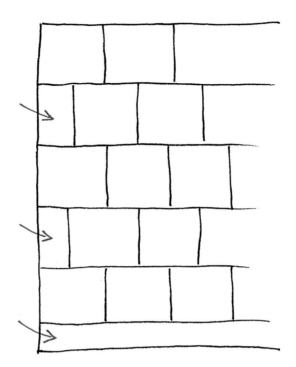

Stagger the block arrangement. Fill in the gaps on the sides.

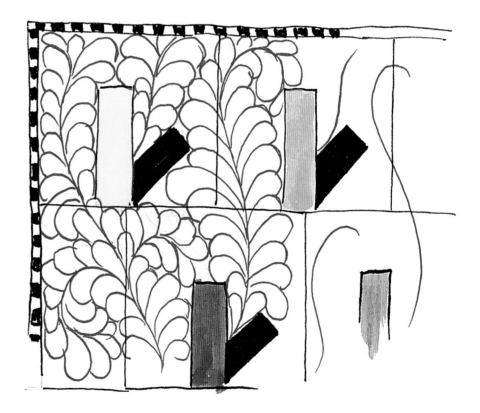

Quilting suggestion.

Starry Sky
2⅜ × 2½ yards (215 × 220 cm)

Stars with rays of differing lengths sparkle and glitter. Each star's center is a different color. You can also switch the yellow tones to create a richly varied starry sky. The complementary colors blue and orange/yellow lend this quilt its radiance.

▤ Materials
Fabrics
- Sample book/books: Cotton, all colors, for ninety 2⅓" × 2⅓" cm (6 × 6 cm) squares.
- 1⅔ yards (1.50 m) total amount of yellow, of various tones, for the rays.
- 8¾ yards (8.00 m) bright blue, solid or lightly patterned, for the sky.

Or alternatively for the star centers:
- a) ⅞ yard (0.70 m) rainbow fabric.
- b) Ombre fabrics: 6" (15 cm) each of red, yellow, blue, green, and brown.
- c) Fabric pack: about twenty assorted solid-colored squares, such as 4¾" × 4¾" (12 × 12 cm) (for four each of similar star centers, 2⅓" × 2⅓" cm [6 × 6 cm])

Other
- Large square ruler (such as 12½" × 12½" [32 × 32 cm]).
- 2⅝ × 2⅝ yards (235 × 240 cm) backing fabric.
- 2⅝ × 2⅝ yards (235 × 240 cm) volume fleece.
- Dark-blue quilting thread.
- 9⅞ yards (9.00 m) egg yolk yellow bias binding for the binding.

▤ Instructions
90 Star Blocks
(Lesson 1: Basic Shapes,
Lesson 3: Attaching Triangles)
For each star, cut four rectangles

of about 5⅛" × 2¾" (13 × 7 cm) from the blue fabric (total of 360 blue rectangles). Cut out four 4⅓" × 2¾" (11 × 7 cm) rectangles from the yellow fabric (a total of 180 yellow rectangles). Divide two

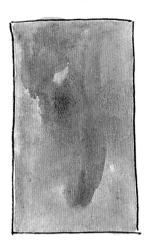

Cut out four blue rectangles (about 5⅛" × 2¾" [13 × 7 cm]) for the background of the star rays.

Square for the star center. The measurement is given in step 7 and matches the short-side length of the ray unit (2⅓" × 2⅓" [6 × 6 cm]).

yellow rectangles along the bias from left to right, and the other two on the bias from right to left. This creates very long right-angled triangles that can be pieced together diametrically opposite.

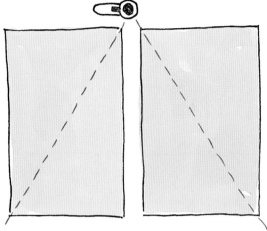

Cut out four yellow rectangles (about 4⅓" × 2¾" [11 × 7 cm]) for the rays; divide two of them on the bias from left to right, and divide the other two on the bias from right to left.

Cut one of the lower corners off a blue rectangle on the bias lengthwise and attach the long edge of a yellow triangle to this cut edge. Smooth the yellow corner to the outside with a fingernail. Then cut the other corner away lengthwise, sew on the diametrically opposite yellow triangle, and press it outward. Cut away unequal corner pieces by design to give the stars the desired sparkle. Sew four such units, each time of the same yellow. Iron the units and trim them to an equal size; here, it is exactly $4\frac{1}{3}$" × $2\frac{1}{3}$" (11 × 6 cm).

Cut four squares of $4\frac{1}{3}$" × $4\frac{1}{3}$" (11 × 11 cm) (total of 360 squares) per block out of the blue fabric. The edge lengths of the squares match the long edge of the just-sewn and trimmed rectangle with the ray (star point unit).

Cut out squares of exactly $2\frac{1}{3}$" × $2\frac{1}{3}$" (6 × 6 cm) per block out of the rainbow fabric (ninety in total). The edge lengths of the squares match the short edge of the previously sewn and trimmed rectangle with the ray.

Piece together the four ray units, the four blue squares, and the center square of a star block. Piece each star block together individually. First sew the two lengthwise seams without cutting the threads between the units. Then join the two crosswise seams. Make a total of ninety star blocks. Iron the seams of two opposite star point units to the center and those of the others outward. Finally, trim all the star blocks to an exactly uniform size; here, it is $9\frac{1}{16}$" × $9\frac{1}{16}$" (23 × 23 cm).

Sewing Plan

Arrange the blocks in ten horizontal rows of nine blocks each. Place each row, with the centers offset, under the previous one. Arrange the stars with bright centers in the middle of the quilt; put the stars with the darker, and thus more contrasting centers, toward the outside. Fill in the gaps on the sides with ten blue rectangles. The measurement for these is half a block width plus seam allowance, and the same height as a star block (here $9\frac{1}{16}$" × 5" [12.5 × 23 cm]). To piece together the quilt top, sew the blocks into rows and then sew the rows on beneath each other.

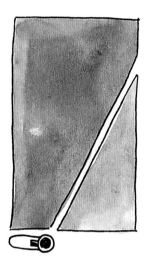

Cut off a lower corner of a blue rectangle on the bias.

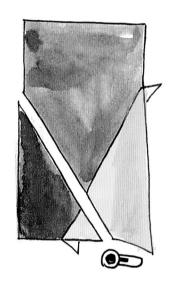

Cut off the other lower corner on the bias.

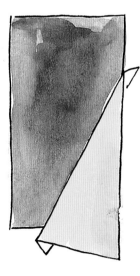

Attach a yellow triangle with the long edge as the star point. Fold the triangle outward.

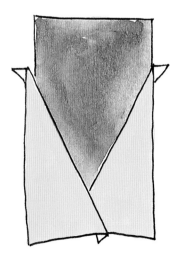

Attach the next yellow triangle with the long edge as the star point. Fold the triangle outward. Iron the point unit and trim precisely ($4\frac{1}{3}$" × $2\frac{1}{3}$" [11 × 6 cm]).

Quilting suggestion.

Piecing a block together: One colored center square (exactly 2¹⁄₃" × 2¹⁄₃" [6 × 6 cm]), four blue corner squares (exactly 4¹⁄₃" × 4¹⁄₃" [11 × 11 cm]), and four star point units (4¹⁄₃" × 2¹⁄₃" [11 × 6 cm]). Piece the block together.

Quilting
(Lessons 11 and 12)
Assemble the ironed backing, volume fleece, and quilt top one atop the other. Use blue quilting thread to quilt a block-sized circle around each star and a second inner circle ¹⁄₃" (1 cm) inside the first. Fill in the gaps in between with a dense surface pattern (here a pebble pattern). Use yellow thread to sew along the points of the star. If you quilt by hand, omit the top pattern and quilt a simple circle around each star.

Binding
(Lesson 13)
Bind the basted edge with an egg yolk yellow bias binding.

Evening Bag
About 4" × 6" (10 × 15 cm)

There is just enough room in this small evening bag for your keys, paper money, a handkerchief, opera glasses, and your coat check token. Sew this elegant evening bag from the squares of silk left over from the Swirl pattern (pages 18–22). It is pieced together based on the "windmill handbag" method; there are instructions for this on the Internet and in many books.

■ Materials
Fabrics (for a single bag)
- Each ⅛ yard (0.12 m) Honan silk in two complementary colors (such as red and green, purple and yellow, or blue and orange).
- ⅓ yard (0.25 m) handbag lining in matching colors, such as Honan silk.

Or as desired
- The same amount of cotton fabric, solid, in complementary colors (see above).

Other
- 8" (0.20 m) very thin iron-on interfacing.
- Some baking paper.
- 4 brass rings, ½" (15 mm) diameter (such as washers from a home improvement store).
- 1⅓ yards (1.20 m) narrow, shiny cord in a matching color.

■ Instructions
16 Squares in Complementary Contrasting Colors
(Lesson 1: Basic Shapes,
Lesson 2: Double Cutting)
Sew sixteen squares with a colored center as described in Lesson 2. Start with squares sized about 4¾" × 4¾" (12 × 12 cm). Iron them—as described for the "Swirl" quilt—onto thin iron-on interfacing to keep the edges from fraying (this step is unnecessary when working with cotton fabrics). Now trim all the squares to the same size; here it is exactly 3⁵⁄₃₂" × 3⁵⁄₃₂" (8 × 8 cm).

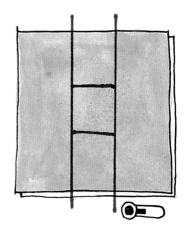

Sew the squares with colored centers together as described for the "Swirl" quilt.

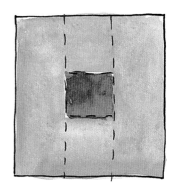

Turquoise with brown center point.

Brown with turquoise center point.

42

Handbag Design

Sew four blocks each into four separate rows, then iron them. For a pattern: put one of these rows on the fabric for the lining and cut out four strips of the same size. Piece the four rows together like a windmill (as illustrated). First sew together the four short edges to make the bottom of the handbag, then fold the side edges over each other and join the side seams. Sew the four stripes of the lining just the same way, but leave 4¾" (12 cm) open on one side seam to be able to turn the handbag inside out later.

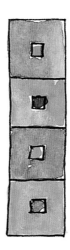

Sew four squares each into four rows.

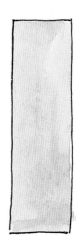

Use one of the pieced-together rows as a measure to make four lining strips.

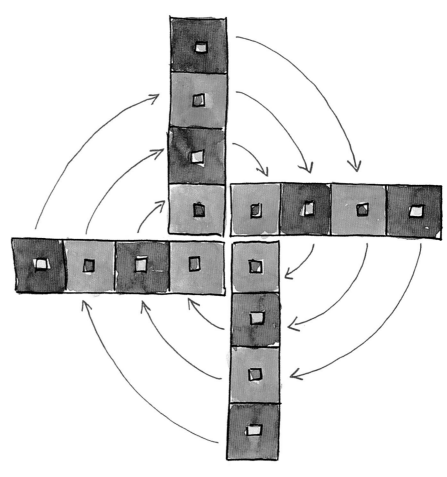

Piece together the four rows of squares into a "windmill" pattern: first, the bottom (here the four turquoise squares), then join the side seams. Piece the four lining strips together in a "windmill" the same way. Join the bottom and side seams, while leaving an opening for turning the handbag inside out.

Opening for Turning

Slip the handbag lining—right sides facing—into the outer handbag. Match the points exactly with each other. Sew at the seam allowance width along the four points. Notch the seam allowance in the corners and trim away the seam allowance at the tips. Turn the handbag out through the opening in the lining. Carefully press out the tips and iron the points.

Either close the turning opening by hand or make a narrow seam by machine. Slip the lining back into the handbag.

Finishing

Sew a brass ring between each of the points in the top. Divide the cord into two equal lengths. Thread each through the four rings and tie the ends of each separate cord together. This lets you close your small evening bag.

TIP

You can also change the size of the bag by sewing only three squares into the rows, or you can make double rows for an even-larger bag.

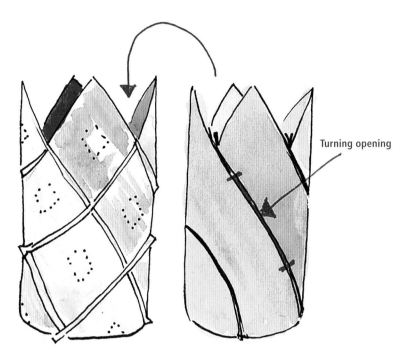

Turning opening

Slip the two bags one into the other, right sides facing, and sew the pointed upper edges together.

How to turn the tips of the seam allowances and trim the angle back to the seam.

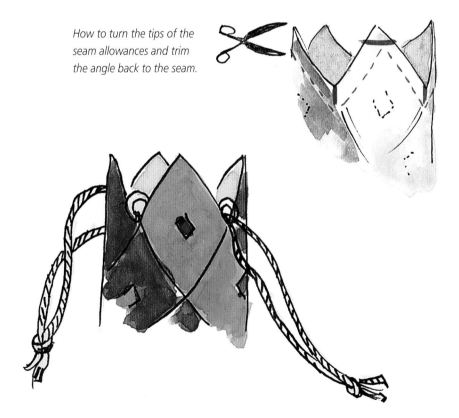

Turn the handbag right side out through the opening in the lining, then press out the points and iron them. Sew a brass ring between each of the points. Pull the two cords through the rings and knot each individually.

45

M-stars
1½ × 1⅓ yards (135 × 118 cm)

You can draw fine contours using inset lines. Four four-patch blocks, with the lines forming an "M" in each, create a dainty star when pieced together. The sashings visually separate the stars from each other. I wish we had more fabric squares, because this would have also made a beautiful bed quilt.

▥ Materials
Fabric

- Sample book with at least eighty different solid colors, each about 6⅓" × 6⅓" (16 × 16 cm); separate out any very light fabrics.
- 2¼ yards (2.00 m) natural white (fine muslin) for the lines, the sashings, and the inner borders.
- 2" (0.05 m) petrol green for the cornerstones.
- ⅝ yards (0.50 m) bright coral for the outer border.

Or as desired

- A range of Amish fabrics, at least eighty squares, 6⅓" × 6⅓" (16 × 16 cm); separate out any very light fabrics.
- ⅜ yard (0.35 m) ombre fabrics of six different colors; separate out any very light tones.
- 2¼ yards (2.00 m) rainbow fabric.

Other

- 1⅔ × 1½ yards (150 × 130 cm) backing fabric.
- 1⅔ × 1½ yards (150 × 130 cm) volume fleece.
- Coral and cream-white quilting thread.
- 5¾ yards (5.20 m) red bias binding for the binding (a bit darker than the outer border).

▥ Instructions
Cutting Out

Cut the muslin into 1"-wide (2.5 cm) strips to make the lines. Use a ruler, but you do not need to measure accurately to the millimeter.

Cut the colored fabrics into squares of 6⅓" × 6⅓" (16 × 16 cm). The sashings, also of muslin, should be cut to exactly 2" (5 cm) width, and the petrol green cornerstones to exactly 2" × 2" (5 × 5 cm).

Cut through a square (about 6⅓" × 6⅓" [16 × 16 cm]) once lengthwise and then across the center. Cut through the two opposite squares on the bias.

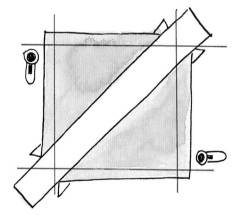

2 × block A: Sew one light strip about 1" (2.5 cm) wide between the diagonals of the two cut-through squares. Trim to exactly 2⅓" × 2⅓" (6 × 6 cm).

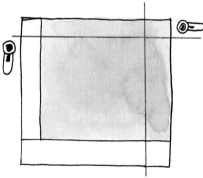

1 × block B: Sew one muslin strip each to two adjacent edges. Trim to exactly 2⅓" × 2⅓" (6 × 6 cm), leaving the muslin strip intact. Cut block C likewise to 2⅓" × 2⅓" (6 × 6 cm).

80 M-blocks

Divide each of the solid squares once lengthwise and once crosswise into four equal sections; here, they measure 3⁵⁄₃₂" × 3⁵⁄₃₂" (8 × 8 cm). Divide two opposite squares once on the bias.

In each diagonal, inset a strip of muslin and iron the seam allowances away from the strip (square A). On the upper-right square, sew a muslin strip to each of two adjacent edges (square B). Square C remains as is.

Now trim the four squares to the same size; here, it is exactly 2¾" × 2¾" (7 × 7 cm). Start with square A and place the square ruler so that the diagonal line of the ruler lies centrally on the diagonal line of the block. For square B, place the square ruler so that little or nothing will be trimmed from the muslin strips, and most will be trimmed from the colored fabric. Also trim square C to 2¾" × 2¾" (7 × 7 cm).

Piece together all four blocks into an "M" and join the seams.

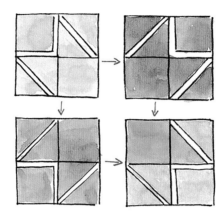

Piece together four M-blocks and join the seams.

TIP
If the colored fabrics are significantly sturdier than the fabric for the lines, you should iron the seam allowances toward the inset line. They will overlap somewhat there, but there is no alternative. When you piece together the entire star, you should iron the seam allowances of the lengthwise and crosswise seams apart to avoid very thick seams.

Sew the four squares into a four-patch block, in which the lines form an "M." Iron the block and, if necessary, trim it to exactly 4¾" × 4¾" (12 × 12 cm). Sew at least eighty M-blocks. It is a good idea to have some "M's" in reserve so you can switch the colors.

20 Star Blocks
Sort four color coordinated M-blocks into one star and sew together. The finished star is now about 8½" × 8½" (22 × 22 cm). Sew twenty stars.

Piecing the Quilt Together
(Lesson 9)
Make five horizontal rows of four
stars each. Add the thirty-one
muslin sashings (exactly 2" [5
cm] wide) with each strip as long
as the star; here, it is 8½" (22 cm).

At the intersections, insert
twelve petrol green cornerstones
of exactly 2" × 2" (5 × 5 cm).

Piece the quilt top together.

Outer Borders
(Lesson 10)
Inner border strips, muslin, 2" (5
cm) cutting width, four
cornerstones.

Outer border strips, coral, 4"
(10 cm) cutting width, straight
corners.

Quilting
(Lessons 11 and 12)
Assemble the backing, volume
fleece, and quilt top one atop the
other. Use cream-white quilting
thread to quilt a border design
along the lines and sashings, and
an orange peel pattern on the
middle block intersection of the
stars. If you quilt by hand, you
can match the quilting thread
color to the color of the star. Use
red thread to quilt a border
design with lines running
outward (piano key pattern) on
the wide border.

Binding
(Lesson 13)
Bind the quilt edge with red bias
binding.

Arrangement of the blocks and sashing with cornerstones and two borders.

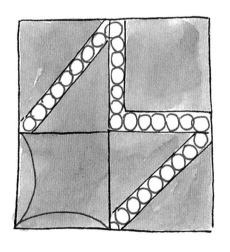

Quilting suggestion for the M-blocks.

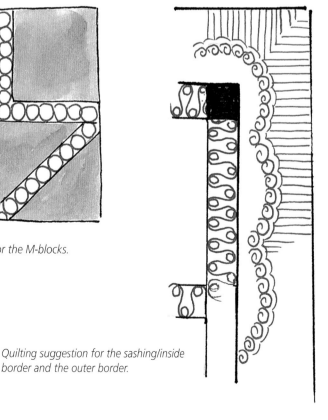

Quilting suggestion for the sashing/inside border and the outer border.

M-star Cushion
20" × 20" (50 × 50 cm) each

Do you have extra M-star blocks left over? Are there some nice fabric squares lying around uselessly? Sew some cushions in sweet candy colors, or other colors that go with your furnishings.

▨ Materials
Fabric per cushion
- ¼ yard (0.20 m) color 1, solid, or four color-matched squares 6⅓" × 6⅓" (16 × 16 cm) each for the M-blocks.
- 2" (0.05 m) black-and-white-striped fabric, stripe width about ¼" (6 mm), for the piping.
- 4" (0.10 m) muslin for the lines and the inner border strips.
- 2" (0.05 m) color 2, solid, for the cornerstones (or four 2" × 2" [5 × 5 cm] squares).
- ⅓ yard (0.25 m) color 3, solid, for the outer border.

Other per cushion
- ⅝ × ⅝ yards (55 × 55 cm) fabric for the cushion linings.
- ⅝ × ⅝ yards (55 × 55) cm volume fleece.
- ⅝ × ¾ yards (55 × 65) cm matching color for cushion backing.
- cream white quilting thread.
- 20" × 20" (50 × 50 cm) cushion filling.
- 15¾" (40 cm) matching color zipper.

▨ Instructions
The inner border strips of muslin should be exactly 2" (5 cm) wide, and the cornerstones exactly 2" × 2" (5 × 5 cm). Use a ruler, but you do not need to measure accurately to the millimeter.

4 M-blocks
Cut the color 1 fabric into squares of approximately 6⅓" × 6⅓" (16 × 16 cm). Cut the muslin into 1" (2.5 cm) wide strips for the M-lines. Sew four M-blocks as described for the "M-star" quilt. Piece these four blocks together to form a star. If necessary, straighten the outer edges.

Borders
(Lesson 10)
1. Piping strip: exactly 1" (2.5 cm) cut width, folded lengthwise, sewn directly to the star block.
2. Inner borders: muslin, 2" (5 cm) cutting width, with 2" × 2" (5 × 5 cm) cornerstones in color 2.
3. Outer border strips, color 3, 4¾" (12 cm) cutting width, straight corners.

Quilting
(Lessons 11 and 12)
Assemble the backing, volume fleece, and quilt top one atop the other. Quilt with a cream-white thread along the lines and on the inner border strips, once each close to the edge on the outer edges and once about ⅓" (1 cm) from the piping strip. Quilt a pattern you like on the wide border; here it is loops and piano keys.

Sewing the Pillow
(Lesson 14)
Sew a zipper into the pillow back and finish the cushion.

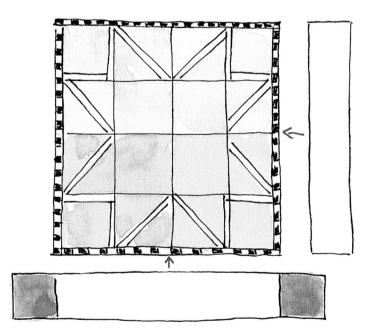

Sew together the M-blocks as described for the M-star quilt (see page 48) and piece it together to form a star block. Fold the black and white piping (1" [2.5 cm] cutting width) and stitch inside the seam allowance around the block. Attach the cornerstones (2" × 2" [5 × 5 cm]) to the inside border (2" [5 cm] cutting width). Finally, sew on the wide colored border.

LOG CABIN PATTERN

Lesson 4:
Log Cabin
Projects: Strange Birds,
Seersucker Log Cabin, Red Flowers,
Spring Sun, Jeans plus Jeans

You can sew several log cabin blocks simultaneously or each block individually. In either case, follow the same rules. Start with a center square in the desired size and cut the fabric into strips in the width specified in the project. You can cut the strips exactly or freehand. Pay attention to the specified color sequence. For some projects there may even be a different sewing sequence.

Sewing a Log Cabin Block
(To illustrate the rounds the same color was used each time.)
Cut out a center square.

First Round
Place the strips for the first round under the presser foot, right side up. Place the center square, right sides facing, along the strip and sew along the right edge at presser foot width. Trim the strip along the lower edge of the center square. Unfold the sewn-on strip and iron it outward.

> **TIP**
> You might want to iron the pieces first and then cut the units from the strip; the result is the same. Perhaps a bit more exact?

Place the strip for the second edge under the presser foot, right side up. Place the first pieced-together unit, right sides facing,

on the strip, with the center square pointing upward. Sew along the right edge. Trim the strip along the lower edge of the unit. Unfold the sewn-on strip and press it outward.

Place the strip for the third edge under the presser foot, right

side up. Place the first pieced-together unit, right sides facing, on the strip, with the center square facing upward. Sew along the right edge. Trim the strip along the lower edge of the unit. Unfold the sewn-on strip and press it outward.

Center square.

Have the strip color for round 1 ready. Lay the center square, right sides facing, on the strip. Sew the right edge. Cut off the strip protruding below. Unfold and iron.

Turn the unit so that the center square faces upward. Lay the center square, right sides facing, on the strip. Sew the right edge. Cut off the strip protruding below. Unfold and iron.

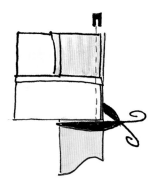

Turn the unit so that the center square faces upward. Lay the center square, right sides facing, on the strip. Sew the right edge. Cut off the strip protruding below. Unfold and iron.

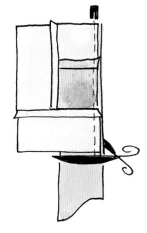

Turn the unit so that the edge with the two seams faces to the right. Lay the center square, right sides facing, on the strip. Sew the right edge. Cut off the strip protruding below. Unfold and iron.

Put the unit to the left of your sewing machine, fabric right side down. The edge with two short seams faces to the right of the sewing machine.

Place the strip for the fourth edge under the presser foot, right side up. Place the pieced-together unit, right sides facing, so that the edge with the two seams faces to the right. Sew along the right edge. Trim the strip along the lower edge of the unit. Unfold the sewn-on strip and iron it outward. The first round is sewn.

Second Round

From now on, always place the unit on the next strip, so that the edge with two short cross seams faces to the right.

Have the strips for the second round ready, and place the unit on them so that the edge with the two seams faces to the right. Sew the unit to the strip and cut it off along the lower edge. Unfold the sewn-on strip and iron it outward.

All the following steps are the same; the next strip is always attached to the edge with two short cross seams.

All the strips, and thus all the seam allowances, are ironed outward. Finally, use a square ruler to again trim all the blocks exactly to a uniform size.

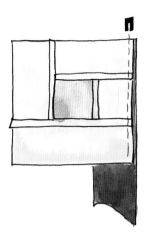

Have the strip color for round 2 ready. Turn the unit so that the edge with the two seams faces to the right. Lay the center square, right sides facing, on the strip. Sew the right edge. Cut off the strip protruding below. Unfold and iron.

Turn the unit so that the edge with the two seams faces to the right. Lay the center square, right sides facing, on the strip. Sew the right edge. Cut off the strip protruding below. Unfold and iron. Continue working in this way until all rounds are sewn on.

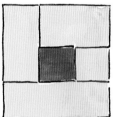

Round 1 is sewn (same stripe color all around).

Rounds 1 and 2 are sewn.

Rounds 1, 2, and 3 are sewn.

Log Cabin

Lesson 5:
Adhesive Applique
Projects: Strange Birds, Bird Cushions

This is a creative method for adhesive applique where you work without stencils. It works well for very small pieces of fabric and for free-form designs, such as birds, flowers, and leaves.

TIP
The "classic" method would be to work with stencils so that you transfer the outline, mirror inverted, on the paper side of the adhesive fleece, cut it out roughly, and then iron it on the wrong side of the fabric and cut out the shape exactly along the lines.

Preparing the Fabric
Lay a larger piece of adhesive fleece, with the adhesive side up, on an ironing board and place your pieces of fabric close together on it, wrong side down. Spread over a sheet of baking paper and iron, hot and dry. As soon as the material sticks remove the baking paper. Let the fabric cool. Then cut out the fabric pieces together with the paper layer, and trim off the protruding paper edges up to the fabric. For the next pieces of fabric, use a fresh area of the baking paper, since a lot of the adhesive will remain stuck to it.

You now have many pieces of fabric with the adhesive fleece paper layer attached to the wrong side. It is easy to cut the designs out from these reinforced fabric pieces with scissors. Keep the designs simple and choose clear shapes.

Cutting Out the Designs
Select a fabric color and cut out a motif or motif section. It is practical to cut out directly from the fabric side, because you do not need to reflect the design and you can allow for suitable printed patterns.

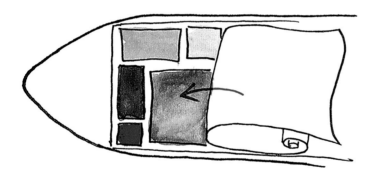

Iron pieces of fabric to the adhesive fleece with the aid of baking paper laid on top of the adhesive side.

Cut out the fabric pieces individually and keep them ready.

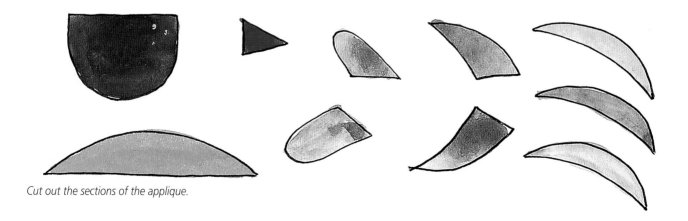

Cut out the sections of the applique.

Adhesive Applique

Laying Out the Applique

When you have placed all the sections of the desired motif on the background, pick up the applique section again. Use a needle or the tip of a scissor blade to slit the paper layer in the center. Now it is easy to grasp the paper and pull it away. This way, you do not ruin the edge. Place the fabric, with the now-exposed adhesive side, back on the background fabric.

Ironing On the Applique

Arrange all the cut-out sections of the motif again on the background fabric. Take note of what section has to lie on top of or underneath another section, then spread baking paper over it again and iron hot and dry until all the pieces of fabric adhere firmly. Let the fabric cool.

Stitching around the Applique

You need an additional step to attach these pieces of fabric, because otherwise they will come off when washed. Therefore, sew around the edges using the freehand embroidery technique (Lesson 8: Freehand Embroidery), or by machine using one of your sewing machine's decorative stitches.

TIP

Anyone who has trouble with "freehand embroidery" should use a sewing machine. Turn the fabric in the respective sewing direction and work several times around the shapes. Do not use an upper fabric mover.

Arrange the individual sections on the background fabric. Each time pull off the backing paper from the wrong side. Place the fabric pieces back in their original positions. Pay attention to what is "on top" and "underneath." Spread some baking paper on the applique and iron the fabric pieces fast. Sew around the edges.

Lesson 6:
Accent Stripes

Cut out your accent stripes precisely with a ruler and sew them at presser foot width. Use two fabrics with a strong color contrast, such as black and white, orange and blue, light green and pink, etc.

Cut out several stripes of equal width from the contrasting fabrics, such as two stripes each from the white-and-black fabric, of exactly 2" (5 cm) width.

Sew the stripes together along the long edges, switching the colors. Divide these sewn bands in four and piece them together as before, along their lengthwise edges. Always iron the seam allowance to the dark fabric.

TIP
Do not sew these units any wider than 23⅝" (60 cm) so you can still use a quilting ruler.

Cut out several sections of this pieced-together fabric, mostly of the same width as the first fabric stripes you cut. Piece them together into a long band that is long enough for the entire planned length.

Cut the stripes and sew them next to each other on the lengthwise side. Cut the sections as wide as the cutting width of the stripes of fabric.

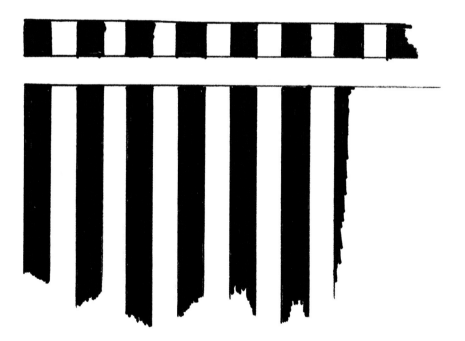

Piece together the sections into a long strip.

TIP
Ready-made printed striped fabrics also work well for accent stripes.

Piping as an Accent

If you want to sew piping into a seam, you need to cut it exactly with a ruler. Usually the strip of piping is cut ¾" (2 cm) (very narrow) or 1" (2.5 cm) (slightly wider) wide. Fold it lengthways, wrong sides facing, and iron it. Sew the strip very close to the quilt or cushion edges—that is, within the seam allowance. The corners of piping should overlap. Then add the outer border strips or binding. Some 5⁄64–⅛" (2–3 mm) of the piping will be visible, and the effect is fantastic.

Fold the piping strip (¾–1" [2–2.5 cm] cutting width) lengthwise and sew inside the seam allowance onto the appropriate edges.

Accent Stripes

Shadow Boxes
2½ × 2¼ yards (225 × 195 cm)

Shadows do not necessarily have to be black; here they are purple and aubergine. Match the shadow color to that of the square; the shadow must be significantly darker than the square. It is also important to use light background fabric so that the squares really "fly."

■ Materials
Fabric

- nineteen pre-cut strips, assorted by color, 2.5" (6.5 cm) wide— preferably dotted—for the squares.
- ⅞ yard (0.70 m) purple for the shadows of the light to medium squares.
- ⅓ yard (0.25 m) dark aubergine for the shadows of the medium-dark squares.
- ⅓ yard (0.25 m) black for the shadows of the darkest squares.
- 9⅞ yards (9.00 m) pure white for the background.
- ⅔ yard (0.60 m) striped black and white (stripe width of about ⅓" [1 cm]) for the binding.

Or alternatively for the squares
- 1⅔ yards (1.50 m) rainbow fabric, preferably dotted.
- Fabric pack/packs of about eighty assorted colored squares of 4¾" × 4¾" (12 × 12 cm) for four equal squares each of about 2⅓" × 2⅓" (6 × 6 cm). Leave out white and other very light fabrics.
- Sample book/books, enough for 288 squares of 2½" × 2½" (6.5 × 6.5 cm). Leave out white and other very light fabrics.

Other
- 2⅝ × 2½ yards (240 × 220 cm) backing fabric.
- 2⅝ × 2½ yards (240 × 220 cm) volume fleece.
- White quilting thread.

■ Instructions
Cutting Out
(Lesson 1: Basic Shapes)
Use precut strips or cut strips of rainbow fabric of about 2.5" (6.5 cm) wide, selvedge to selvedge. Use a ruler, but you do not need to measure accurately to the millimeter. Divide each strip into squares of about 2½" × 2½" (6.5 × 6.5 cm). You need 288 squares.

> **TIP**
>
> If you use precut strips, first cut away the selvedge from the short end of a strip. Take this piece and place it along the long edge of the strip. This gives you a measurement for the squares and you do not need a ruler at all.

From the purple, aubergine, and black fabrics, cut out ten strips of 2" (5 cm) and ten strips of about 2¾" (7 cm) wide, selvedge to selvedge, for the shadows. You will also need twenty strips of pure white of about 1¼" (3 cm) cutting width.

Calculation
You can cut two 2"-wide (5 cm) and two 2¾"-wide (7 cm) strips from a ⅓ yard-wide (0.25 m) piece of fabric.

Cut out about 150 strips of 2⅓" (6 cm) width from the white fabric to surround the "flying" squares.

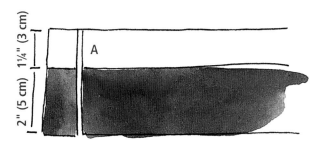

A units: For each, sew a white strip 1¼" (3 cm) and a dark strip (2" [5 cm]) together lengthwise. Cut sections out 1¼" (3 cm) wide.

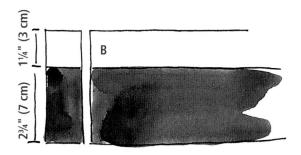

B units: For each, sew a white strip (1¼" [3 cm]) and a dark strip (2" [5 cm]) together lengthwise. Cut sections out 1¼" (3 cm) wide.

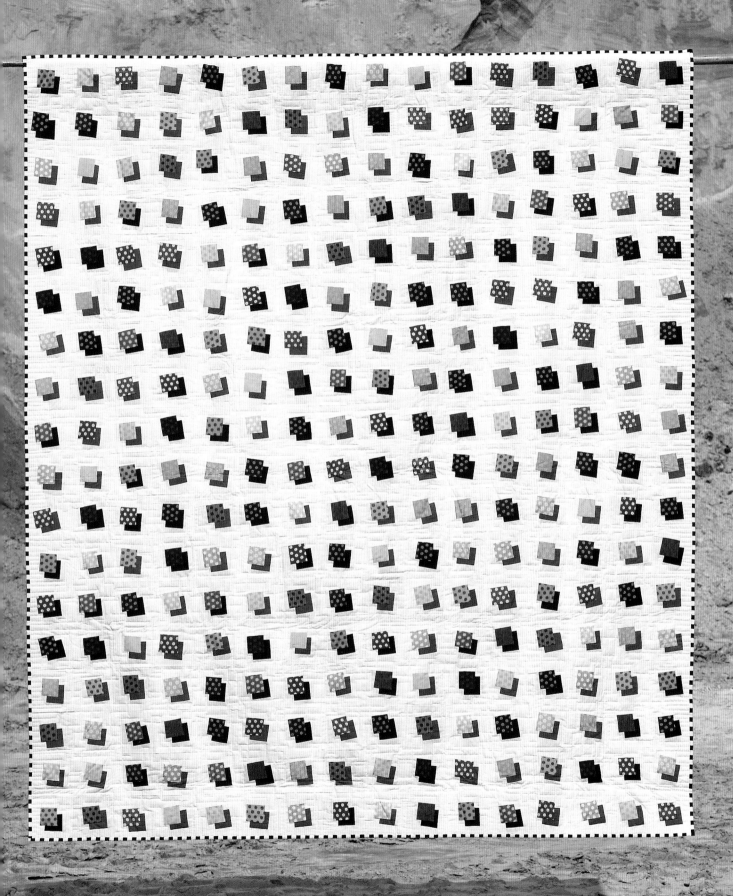

Sewing the Shadow Units

Sew a white strip each time to the lengthwise edge of the dark shadow strips, and iron the seam allowance toward the dark fabric. Trim the units 1¼" (3 cm) wide as illustrated. Use a ruler to cut them out, but you do not need to measure accurately to the millimeter. You need 288 shorter A units and 288 longer B units.

Sew 288 "Flying" Shadow Box Blocks

(Lesson 4: Log Cabin)

First round (half): Sew one each of a short unit and a longer unit to two adjacent edges of a square. The dark ends meet at the corner. You now have sewn a half "log cabin" round. Iron after each seam. Press the seam allowances toward the center square.

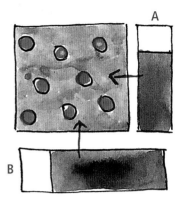

1st round (half): first attach unit A, then unit B to the colored square (2½" × 2½" [6.5 × 6.5 cm]).

Example: Move unit A unit slightly back to the left.

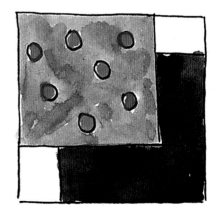

Finished round 1. The dark ends meet at the corner.

2nd round: Sew the white stripes around the square.

Second round: Sew the 2⅓"-wide (6 cm) white stripe around the resulting block center. After each seam, iron the seam allowance outward.

> **TIP**
> When you lay the patchwork block, right sides facing, on the white strip, slide the colored fabric about 1 mm to the left so that the white fabric sticks out a bit to the right. This way, after ironing, the dark fabric edges will not show through to the quilt top.

Using a square ruler, cut all the blocks to a uniform size; here, it is exactly 5½" × 5½" (14 × 14 cm). The white background is wide enough so that you can set the square ruler at a diagonal each time. This gives you edgy, lively floating squares. Of course, you also have individual "straight" flying squares.

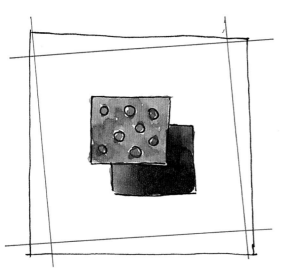

Place the square ruler slanting at an angle to the left and cut out the block (here 5½" × 5½" [14 × 14 cm]).

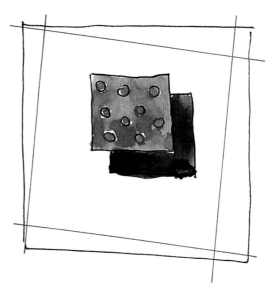

Place the square ruler slanting at an angle to the right and cut out the block (here 5½" × 5½" [14 × 14 cm]).

Sew the extra blocks into a nice cushion.

Piecing the Quilt Together
(Lesson 9)

Arrange the blocks so that the colors appear as if they are distributed randomly. Make sure that the shadow is always to the same side. Arrange eighteen horizontal rows of eighteen blocks each one above the other. Piece the blocks together for the quilt top.

Quilting
(Lessons 11 and 12)

Assemble the backing, volume fleece, and quilt top one atop the other. Use white thread to quilt overlapping horizontal lines and vertical meanders on the white areas. Leave the squares and shadows untouched.

Binding
(Lesson 13)

Bind the quilt edge with a black-and-white-striped, straight-cut, doubled strip of fabric, cutting width 2⅓" (6 cm).

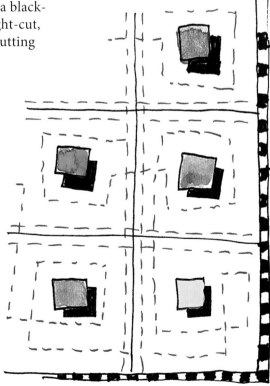

Border design and quilting suggestion. All the shadows should point in the same direction.

Strange Birds
2⅓ × 2¼ yards (208 × 195 cm)

The birds' overlong legs make them look really "weird." Rummage through your snippets box and use all the bright fabrics you have, especially dotted ones. The log cabin blocks are made from the usual strips, but also from pieced-together strip units, giving an interesting restlessness to the green areas.

▥ Materials
Fabric
- ⅔ yard (0.60 m) light blue for the border of birds.
- ⅓ yard (0.25 m) wine red for the block centers.
- 2¾ yards (2.50 m) various light blue tones for the blue quarter of the block.

- 2¾ yards (2.50 m) various soft yellows for the yellow quarter of the block.
- 5½ yards (5.00 m) (total) of different medium-green, yellow-green, and blue-green shades for the green-colored block halves (optionally precut strips of Pops, Jelly Rolls, Rollimops, etc.).
- 4" (0.10 m) each white and black, solid, for the accent stripes.

Fabrics for the Birds
- ⅝ yard (0.50 m) (estimated total amount) different fabric remnants in bold colors, small pieces, solid or printed. Dotted fabrics work particularly well.

Other
- Large square ruler (such as 12½" × 12½" [32 × 32 cm]).

- ⅞ yard (0.80 m) iron-on adhesive fleece, both sides adhesive.
- 3' (1.00 m) baking paper.
- Dark-gray sewing thread for embroidery.
- Possibly 1⅛ yard (1.00 m) thin, iron-on volume fleece.
- Possibly an embroidery hoop for the sewing machine.
- Embroidery foot (darning foot/ freehand quilting foot) for the sewing machine.
- 2½ × 2½ yards (220 × 220 cm) backing fabric.
- 2½ × 2½ yards (220 × 220 cm) volume fleece.
- Quilting thread in light yellow, light blue, and acid green.
- 27' (820 cm) tomato-red bias binding for the binding.

▦ Instructions
Cutting Out
(Lesson 1: Basic Shapes)

For the green block halves, cut strips of about 1¼", 1½", and 2⅓" (3, 4, and 6 cm) wide (you could use cloth pack strips). Make the strip sections about 20" (50 cm) wide by sewing the other fabrics, in various colors and widths, to the long edges. Iron the seam allowances together in one direction. Cut units of about 1½" (4 cm) wide from this strip section. This is what is used to make the green colored halves of the log cabin blocks.

Cut seventy-two squares of approximately 2" × 2" (5 × 5 cm) in wine red for the centers, and use a ruler to cut the light yellow and light-blue fabrics into strips 2" (5 cm) wide. You do not have to measure accurately.

36 A Blocks
(Lesson 4: Log Cabin)

Start with a red center square and sew the light-blue fabric to the first side, sew yellow to the second side, and a green pieced-together strip to each of the remaining two edges. Work three rounds, with the same colors matching up each time. Iron all the blocks and trim them to a uniform size; here, it is exactly 9½" × 9½" (24 × 24 cm).

Log cabin block A: Red center, section 1 blue, section 2 yellow, and sections 3 and 4 green colors.

36 B Blocks
(Lesson 4: Log Cabin)

Start with a red center square and sew the light-blue fabric to the first side, fold the strip outward, and place the unit on your machine so that the center square faces downward (!). Sew a yellow strip to the second edge and a green pieced-together strip to each of the remaining two edges. Work three rounds, with the same colors matching up each time. Iron all the blocks and trim them to a uniform size; here, it is exactly 9½" × 9½" (24 × 24 cm).

Log cabin block B: Red center, section 1 blue, section 2 yellow, and sections 3 and 4 green colors. When sewing, pay attention to the position of the center block!

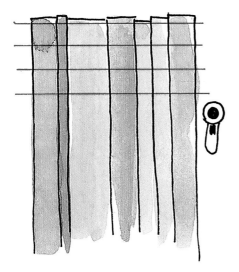

Sew on the green-colored strip sections in different widths. Cut out units of about 1½" (4 cm) wide.

Thirty-six A blocks, sew three rounds, trim exactly (9½" × 9½" [24 × 24 cm]).

Thirty-six B blocks, sew three rounds, trim exactly (9½" × 9½" [24 × 24 cm]).

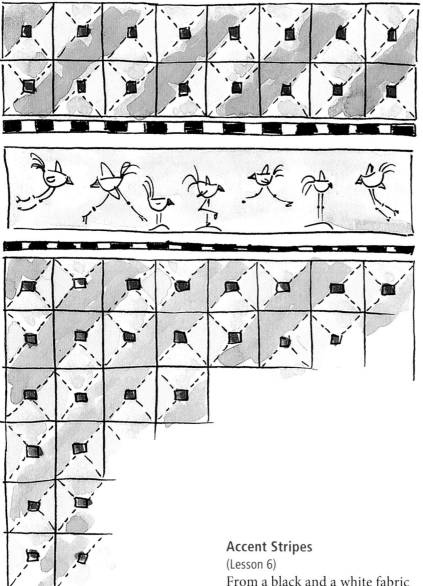

Arrangement of section A (top) and section B (bottom). Sew on the accent stripes; make the stripes exactly 3" (7.5 cm) (cutting width). Sections are exactly 1³⁄₈" (3.5 cm). Attach the accent stripes to sections A and B. Insert the finished border of birds in between.

Border of Birds

(Lesson 5: Adhesive Applique, Lesson 8: Freehand Embroidery)

For the background for Strange Birds, cut out a light-blue strip as wide as the quilt (here 2¼ yards [200 cm]) and 12" (30 cm) high. Iron the thin iron-on volume fleece to the wrong side of the strip. This makes it easier to do the freehand embroidery on the sewing machine (if you are longarm quilting this step is unnecessary).

Place a large piece of adhesive fleece (for example, 12" × 15¾" [30 × 40 cm]), with the adhesive side up, on an ironing board and place your fabric snippets, wrong side down, close together on the adhesive side. Spread a sheet of baking paper over it and iron, hot and dry. As soon as the material sticks remove the baking paper. Cut out the fabric pieces along with the paper layer.

Decide on a color and cut out the bird's body. You can do this "off the cuff," or you can make a simple stencil from cardboard. It is practical to cut out directly from the fabric side. A bird's body should be about 4" (10 cm) long and 3¼" (8 cm) high.

Then cut out the wings from another matching fabric (about 2–2¾" [5–7 cm) long and 1¼–1½" [3–4) cm wide), as well as the beak (small red triangle) and three colorful, crescent-shaped tail feathers (2⅓–3¼" [6–8 cm] long).

Piecing the Quilt Together

(Lesson 9)

The upper section A consists of two rows of nine blocks each, and the lower section B of six rows of nine blocks each. The green colored block halves should form a diagonal from bottom left to top right. Piece together quilt sections A and B as described in Lesson 9.

Accent Stripes

(Lesson 6)

From a black and a white fabric strip, each exactly 3" (7.5 cm) wide, make two accent stripes about 78¾" (200 cm) long and exactly 1³⁄₈" (3.5 cm) cutting width. Sew a strip to the upper edge of the large block section (B) and the other to the lower edge of the upper block section (A). If necessary, sew some of the seams wider or narrower so that the row ends with a whole black or white piece. Now you know the width of your quilt and can trim your border of birds to the corresponding size.

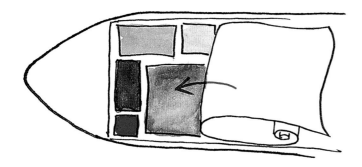

Iron the pieces of fabric to the adhesive side of the adhesive fleece with the aid of baking paper laid on top.

Cut out the fabric pieces individually and keep them ready.

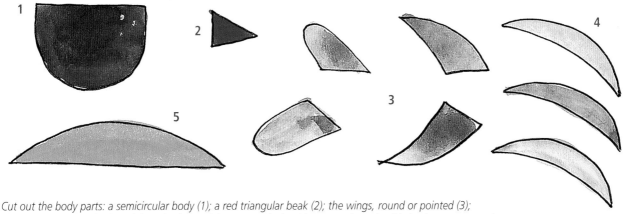

Cut out the body parts: a semicircular body (1); a red triangular beak (2); the wings, round or pointed (3); crescent-shaped tail feathers (4); and a hilltop (5). Remove the backing paper from the fabric pieces, arrange the shapes again, and use a hot iron to iron them fast to the background fabric through a piece of baking paper.

Use pins to mark the positions of the birds on the fabric strips. Make each bird individually. Arrange the bird parts on the background fabric. Check the color effect and the bird's pose. Remove each part and remove the backing paper from the wrong side of the fabric. Put the parts on the background fabric again, as before. Spread baking paper over the birds and iron with a hot iron.

Different poses for the birds.

Embroidering the Applique

Sketch the long legs with chalk or a water soluble pen. Either work "freehand" or stretch the fabric in an embroidery frame so that it runs under the embroidery frame. Now embroider around the contours with dark-gray thread up to three times with the sewing machine; embroider the bird legs the same way. Work the "knee" either as small filled-in circles or (on the sewing machine) using zigzag stitches over a short distance. Embroider loops in between the tail feathers and possibly on the bird's head.

TIP

Anyone who has trouble with "freehand embroidery" can also use a sewing machine. Turn the fabric in the current sewing direction, stitch slowly several times around the shapes, and do not use an upper fabric mover.

Applique six to eight birds, leaving a distance of about 4" (10 cm) between them. Sew the finished border of birds between quilt sections A and B. Iron the seam allowances toward the border of birds.

Sew around the contours of the fabric pieces several times. Also quilt the legs, and quilt loops on the tail feathers. Quilt on the head as well if you like.

TIP for Longarm Quilting

Glue the pieces of fabric for the birds on the background strip. Piece together the entire quilt top and then stretch the three layers in the quilting machine. Now draw the legs with a water soluble pen. As part of the quilting process, stitch the contours and the legs of the birds directly through the three layers of the quilt.

Quilting

(Lesson 12)

Log Cabin pattern: Use light-blue thread to quilt the light-blue areas by hand or with a sewing machine; use yellow thread to quilt leaves in the yellow areas and light-green thread to quilt a feather pattern in the green "crazy" areas.

Border of Birds:

Quilt small upright flowers with long stems on the light-blue background of the bird border, with or without small leaves, and also make some flying insects to decorate the areas between the birds.

Binding

(Lesson 13)

Bind the quilt with wine-red bias binding.

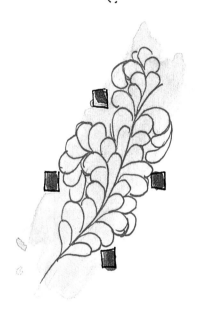

Quilting suggestion for the yellow areas, the light-blue areas, and the green-colored diagonals.

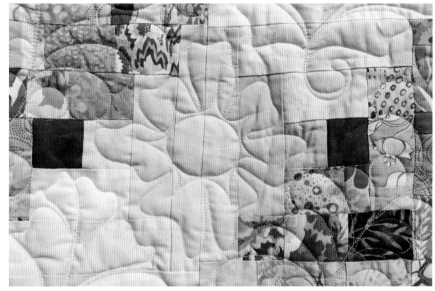

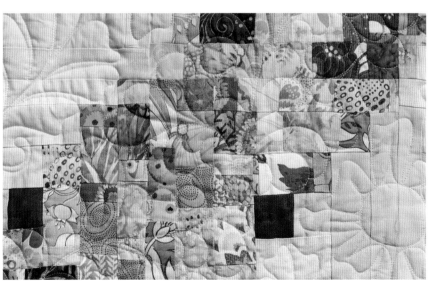

Quilting suggestion for the flowers between the birds.

Springtime Sun
1⅝ × 1¼ yards (148 × 103 cm)

This child's quilt is created using the same sort of log cabin blocks as the "Strange Birds" quilt (pages 63–69).

■ Materials
Fabric
- 4" (0.10 m) wine red for the block centers and inner borders.
- 1⅛ yards (1.00 m) various light-blue tones for the blue quarter of the block.
- 1⅛ yards (1.00 m) various soft yellows for the yellow quarter of the block.
- 2¾ yards (2.50 m) total amount green, different tones, densely printed green, yellow-green, and blue-green for the green-colored block halves and outside border.

Or alternatively for the green color areas:
- At least thirty precut strips 2½" (6.5 cm) wide.

Other
- Large square ruler (such as 12½" × 12½" [32 × 32 cm]).
- 1¾ × 1⅓ yards (160 × 120 cm) backing fabric.
- 1¾ × 1⅓ yards (160 × 120 cm) volume fleece.
- Light-yellow and green-colored quilting thread.
- A CD as a circle pattern.
- 17' (520 cm) green bias binding for the binding.

■ Instructions
Crazy Strip Areas
Sew the green and green-colored fabric into strip units as described for the "Strange Birds" quilt (see page 64). Cut off a 1½"-wide (4 cm) strip.

24 Log Cabin Blocks
(Lesson 4: Log Cabin)
Sew twelve A blocks and twelve B blocks as described for the "Strange Birds" quilt (see page 64). Each block has a wine-red center, a pale-yellow and a light-blue quarter, and a green-colored half. Iron all the blocks and trim them to a uniform size; here, it is exactly 9½" × 9½" (24 × 24 cm).

Twelve A blocks, sew three rounds, trim exactly (9½" × 9½" [24 × 24 cm]).

Twelve B blocks, sew three rounds, trim exactly (9½" × 9½" [24 × 24 cm]).

Piecing the Quilt Together
(Lesson 9)
Make a quilt top of six horizontal rows of four blocks each. Lay out the blocks so that the green-colored sides are facing each other, and each time form a square standing on a point. Piece the blocks together for the quilt top.

Borders
(Lesson 10)
Border 1: Wine red, 2" (5 cm) cutting width, straight corners. Border 2: The rest of the green-colored strips, maximum possible width (here 2" [5 cm]), straight corners.

Quilting
(Lessons 11 and 12)
Quilt big suns with green multicolor thread in the green areas and use yellow-blue thread in the lighter areas. Match to the motif by quilting half suns on the border and quarter suns on the corners. Sew a leaf border in dark-red thread on the inner border strips and use green-colored thread to make "piano keys" running outward on the outermost border.

TIP
Use a CD as a circle pattern.

Binding
(Lesson 13)
Bind the quilt with a grass-green bias binding.

Bird Cushions
20" × 20" (50 × 50 cm)

These playful birds fit in anywhere. Choose a bright background for the bird and extend the sides of the cushion using colors that match its plumage.

▥ Materials
Fabric
- 9¾" × 21½" (25 × 55 cm) bright, solid for the central strip.
- ⅙ yard (0.15 m) color-matched fabric for the sides.
- ⅛ yard (0.10 m) black-and-white striped for the piping.
- Remnants: dotted, striped, bright cotton fabrics for the bird.

Otherwise per cushion:
- Baking paper.
- Double-sided adhesive fleece.
- Water-soluble pen and spray bottle.
- ⅝ × ⅝ yard (55 × 55 cm) fabric for the cushion lining.
- ⅝ × ⅝ yard (55 × 55 cm) volume fleece.
- ⅝ × ¾ yard (55 × 65 cm) matching color for cushion backing.
- Dark sewing thread for embroidery.
- Matching quilting thread.
- 20" × 20" (50 × 50 cm) cushion filling, 15¾" (40 cm) matching zipper.

▥ Instructions
Bird Applique
(Lesson 6: Adhesive Applique)
Cover the colorful fabric scraps with adhesive fleece as described in Lesson 6. First cut out the body of the bird, then the wings, beak, and some tail feathers from fabrics of other colors.

Bird: Semicircle, about 4" × 4" (10 × 10 cm) to 4¾" × 4¾" (12 × 12 cm).
Wing: about 1¼–2" (3–5 cm) wide, about 3¼–4¾" (8–12 cm) long, rounded or pointed.

Beak: red triangle.
Tail feathers: 4–4¾" (10–12) cm long, crescent shaped.
Hilltop (as desired): about 2" (5 cm) high, 4–7⅞" (10–20 cm) wide.

Arrange the bird pieces on the 9¾" × 21½" (25 × 55 cm) light-colored fabric. Check the color effect and the bird's pose. Iron the pieces down firmly as described in Lesson 6.

Sewing the Cushion Top
Cut two strips (exactly 1" [2.5 cm] wide) from the black-and-white striped fabric and fold them lengthwise, wrong sides facing. As a piping, stitch the two strips as on both lengthwise edges of the bird applique, with the open edges facing outward. Sew them just within the seam allowance. Then attach a 6"-wide (15 cm) piece of fabric to each lengthwise edge. Iron the whole piece, and only now use a water-soluble pen to draw the bird legs and tail decorations.

Quilting
(Lesson 12)
Assemble the cushion lining, fleece, and top together. Use black thread to quilt the overlong legs and design them in different positions. The "knee" can be especially funny if you sew a little bump directly on the knee joint or an appropriate place on the legs. Use thread to draw generous loops between the tail feathers and possibly also around the bird's head. A little hill and small embroidered insects will liven up the areas beneath and around the bird.

Quilt close to the edge outside along the piping and add a favorite pattern on the outer areas. Use a spray bottle to remove the water-soluble lines.

Sewing the Pillows
(Lesson 14)
Sew a matching-colored cushion back with a zipper and finish the cushion.

Iron the bird appliques on the central light-colored strips. Sew piping left and right inside the seam allowance, then each time add on a matching-colored outer fabric.

Jeans plus Jeans
2½ × 2⅛ yards (220 × 187 cm)

In this quilt you can study the effect of chiaroscuro contrast. In the dark section, the white crosses emerge as plus signs and the black lines remain in the background, while in the light section, the plus signs recede and the black lines stand out.

■ Materials
Fabric

- Twelve to fifteen worn pairs of jeans (for about fifty to sixty squares per pair).
- 5½ yards (5.00 m) black-and-white striped fabric, with stripes about 2" (5 cm) wide (this is not always available everywhere; see alternative).

Optional for the striped fabric:
- 4⅜ yards (4.00 m) solid white.
- 4⅜ yards (4.00 m) solid black.

Other
- Soft pencil or pen.
- 2⅝ × 2⅓ yards (240 × 210 cm) volume fleece.
- 2⅝ × 2⅓ yards (240 × 210 cm) backing fabric.
- Blue sewing and quilting thread.
- 28' (850 cm) dark-red bias binding for the binding.

■ Instructions
Preparation

In case you have found a wide-striped black-and-white fabric, measure the width of two stripes, from the start of a white one to the end of a black one. Here, this is 3¾" (9.5 cm). This is the side length for the denim squares.

451 Denim Squares

Cut off the seams, pockets, hems, and waistband from the pairs of jeans. Make a 3¾" × 3¾" (9.5 × 9.5 cm) stencil from cardboard. Using this stencil and a soft pencil or a ballpoint pen, transfer the square shape onto the fabric and cut these squares out with scissors. You do not need to pay attention to the fabric grain. Cut out at least 460 such squares, because having a few more blocks will help with color distribution. Sort the denim squares into several piles, from light to dark.

1 C Block

Put aside a very light denim square (block C) for the lower-right corner of the quilt.

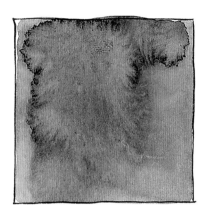

Cut out the denim squares (3¾" × 3¾" [9.5 × 9.5 cm]). Block C consists of a single light square.

41 A Blocks

Cut the black-and-white-striped fabric into crosswise strips 1¼" (3 cm) wide. Divide each white stripe in the middle, giving you pieces with a black center and white ends = segment A. Attach one segment A each to an edge of each denim square. Sew 450 of such A blocks and put aside forty-one very bright A blocks. You need these forty-one for the quilt. Work the remaining 409 A blocks into B blocks.

Cut out sections, each time 1¼" (3 cm) wide, from a fabric with wide stripes (stripe width 2" [5 cm]).

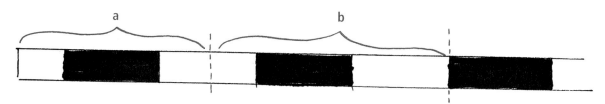

Cut a segment a and segment b from each section.

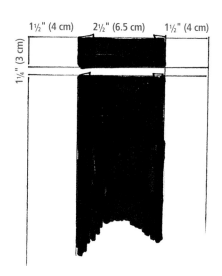

Piecing together the A segments (cutting width as specified). Cut sections 1¼" (3 cm) wide.

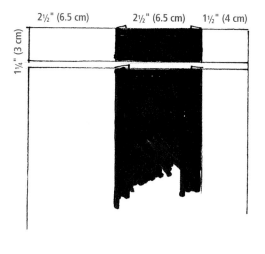

Piecing together the B segments (cutting width as specified). Cut the sections 1¼" (3 cm) wide.

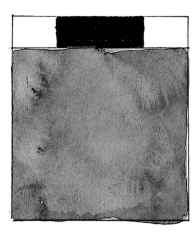

41 × A block, very light blue.

409 B Blocks

Work any leftover A denim squares into B blocks. Cut out pieces from the 1¼"-wide (3 cm) strips that start/end with a complete white stripe and end/start with a half white stripe. Black = segment B, and is in the middle. Add the B segments to an adjacent side of an A denim square, so that the longer white stripe faces the white of the stripe previously sewn on. Sew 409 B blocks.

Piecing the Quilt Together
(Lesson 9)

Piece the quilt top together from twenty-three horizontal rows of twenty blocks each. Start with twenty-two B blocks per row and end each time with an A block, with the sewn-on strips facing underneath. Row 23—the lowest—consists of twenty-two light A blocks that have the sewn-on strips facing right. The last light square (block C) is the one you put aside for the bottom right at the very beginning; now attach it. Piece together the quilt top as described in Lesson 9. Iron all the seam allowances toward the accent stripes.

Quilting
(Lessons 11 and 12)

Use your quilting machine, with blue thread, to quilt on the denim around each square. Alternatively, you could fasten the layers together with knots, such as one knot of blue embroidery thread in each corner of a denim square, or a black or white knot on the sashing.

Binding
(Lesson 13)

Bind the quilt with dark-red bias binding.

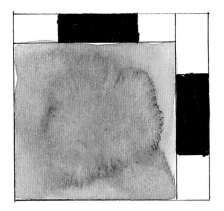

409 B blocks, all shades of blue.

Arrangement of the blocks: Lay the B blocks in a row, and the A blocks to the right at the end of the row (highlighted with green outline). The single light C block is in the lower-right corner. Quilt in the block seams. Bind the edge with red bias binding.

TIP

If you can't find any wide-striped fabric, sew the accent stripes together from black-and-white fabric. Cut black strips (6.5 cm) wide and white strips of 2½" (6.5 cm) and 1½" (4 cm) wide. Make strip A units with a black center stripe, each time with a 1½"-wide (4 cm) white stripe to the right and left. Cut out 1¼" (3 cm) sections = A segments. Make the B strip units with one black center stripe, with a 1½"-wide (4 cm) stripe on one side and a 2½"-wide (6.5 cm) stripe on the other side. Press the seam allowances toward the dark fabric. From these striped units, cut out 1¼" (3 cm) sections = B segments.

Red Flowers
2⅓ × 1⅞ yards (210 × 170 cm)

Packs of pre-cut squares can be used with the freehand cutting technique. Three-dimensional projecting petals make this quilt unique. Do not first look in a store to find the greenish-white fabric for the border triangles; here we simply reworked an old curtain.
Select the flower colors that fit your room: blue with purple or yellow with orange. The effect will be stunning in any case. Moods are expressed by colors. You can also choose other colors for the background. What is important is that there is enough contrast between the flower and the background.

■ Materials
Fabric
- At least 143 assorted 4" × 4" (10 × 10 cm) squares (without red) for the center and round 2.
- 2½ yards (2.20 m) black and white or blue and white narrow striped fabric for rounds 1 and 3.
- 10" × 10" (0.25 m) each (total amount about 2⅞ yards [2.60 m]) various pink- and red-patterned and some turquoise-patterned fabrics for the petals.
- 10" × 10" (0.25 m) each (total amount about 2⅞ yards [2.60 m]) different shades of green, solid, for the backs of the petals.
- 3⅞ yards (3.50 m) bright apricot or natural white for the background.
- 3⅛ yards (2.80 m) pure white for the background.

- ⅞ yard (0.70 m) pale light green, solid or printed with white, for the border triangles.

Or alternatively for the log cabin patch centers:
- Four ombre fabrics, light to dark: ⅝ yard (0.50 m) each in yellow, blue, turquoise, and green.
- 2¼ yards (2.00 m) rainbow fabric (leave out any red tones).

Other
- 2⅝ × 2⅛ yards (230 × 190 cm) backing fabric.
- 2⅝ × 2⅛ yards (230 × 190 cm) volume fleece.
- Bright-red sewing thread.
- Natural-white quilting thread.
- 25½' (780 cm) medium-green bias binding, slightly darker than the border triangles.

■ Instructions
143 Flower Centers

(Lesson 1: Basic Shapes,
Lesson 4: Log Cabin)

Cut out colored squares of about 4" × 4" (10 × 10 cm), or use the convenient precut squares from a fabric pack. Put two distinctly different fabric squares together, the fabric right sides facing upward. Use a rotary cutter, without a ruler, to make three vertical cuts at equal intervals through both layers. You now have four strips (1" [2.5 cm] wide) of each color. Take one strip and cut a square (about 1" × 1" [2.5 × 2.5 cm]) from it. This will be the center square.

Cut the striped fabric into strips about 1" (2.5 cm) wide. Use a ruler, but you do not need to measure accurately to the millimeter.

First Round: Take one of the small center squares and sew a black-and-white-striped piece to all four sides. Iron the seam allowance to the outside.

Second Round: Attach the other four colored stripes from the first step to the center unit. The center should be of another color than in round 2. Start with the shortest strip. Iron the seam allowances to the outside and trim off any protruding ends.

Third round: Again, sew pieces of striped fabric around the center block you are making. Iron the seam allowance to the outside.

Sew at least 143 such log cabin blocks for the flower centers. Having some extra blocks makes it easier when you are later arranging the colors.

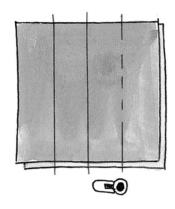

Put two squares (4" × 4" [10 × 10 cm]) one atop the other, both right side up. Make three lengthwise cuts through both layers.

Cut off a small square from one of the resulting strips (about 1" × 1" [2.5 × 2.5 cm]) = center square.

1st round: striped fabric (1" [2.5 cm]) around the center square.

2nd round: colored fabric that contrasts with the center square.

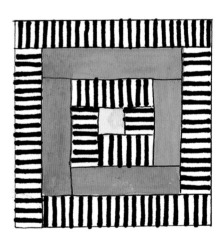

3rd round: striped fabric (1" [2.5 cm]).

143 × 4 Flower Petals

For the petals, prepare the same number of green- and pink/red/orange-patterned strips of fabric, about 2" (5 cm) wide. The green fabric will be used to make the back of the petals. Put one each of the green and red/pink/orange strips, right sides facing, on the cutting mat. Cut sections 3⅓–3½" (8.5–9 cm) long and put the fabrics one atop the other. You should get twelve pieces from one strip, cut selvedge to selvedge. These will make the petals for three flower blocks.

> **TIP**
> You can use shades of green for the backs of the petals. Look through your box of remnants.

Cut out a semicircle through both layers of fabric, which begins and ends at the lower corners, with the center extending to the upper edge. This seems to work better if you use scissors rather than a rotary cutter.

Sew along the semicircle a presser-foot width from the edge. Notch the seam allowances at small intervals close up to the seam—this is easier if the thread color is clearly recognizable—and turn the petal. Iron the semicircular edge. Pin together the four colors that belong together, one atop the other.

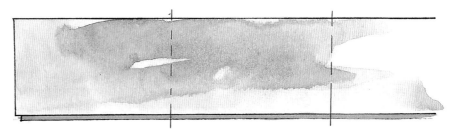

Flower petals: Piece together one each of a green and red fabric strip, of 2" (5 cm) wide, right sides facing. Cut out pieces about 3⅓–3½" (8.5–9 cm) wide.

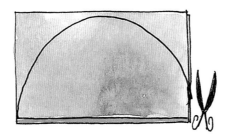

Through both layers of fabric, cut out a semicircle that extends to the corners and the top edge.

Turn the petal, carefully press out the edges, and iron.

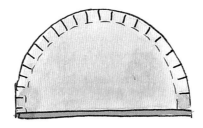

Sew along the semicircle with your sewing machine. Notch the seam allowances at small intervals to close to the seam.

Always pin four similar leaves one atop the other.

> **TIP**
> Pint four similar, stitched semicircles together and collect them in a basket. Then you can notch the seam allowances and turn the petals later on while relaxing (in front of the TV).

143 Flower Blocks

Sort out the matching petals with the log cabin blocks and pin each group to each other. Put light petals on the center blocks with bright and yellow colors. These will later be the A blocks with a white background. Pin dark-red petals to the log cabin blocks of green and darker colors. These will be the B blocks, with the apricot background. The intermediate shades fit in both color groups and make the sorting easier.

Cut the white and apricot background fabrics into squares of about 5½" × 5½" (14 × 14 cm). Divide each square once on the bias into two triangles.

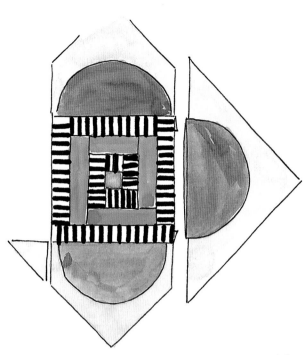

Divide the white (for A blocks) and apricot-colored (for B blocks) squares (5½" × 5½" [14 × 14 cm]) on the bias and sew the resulting triangles around the center unit. Here also set a petal in the seam on each edge, first on two opposite edges, then to the other two edges. Cut away any protruding triangles.

> **TIP**
> You must sew a sample block. It may be that your blocks turn out slightly bigger than you thought, and therefore you will need bigger triangles.

63 A Blocks

Sew the white triangles, each time by its long edge to the four sides of a log cabin center square, and at the same time set a petal into each seam. First sew a triangle onto each of two opposite edges, and then onto the other two opposite edges. Cut off any protruding corners on the wrong side. Iron the seam allowances to the center.

80 B Blocks

Sew four apricot-colored triangles each time around the second group and set the petals into the seam as you did before with the pure white fabrics.

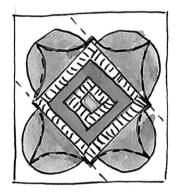

Sixty-three A blocks (white background). Attach the petals to the background with a curving seam. Trim the blocks exactly (5½" × 5½" [14 × 14 cm]).

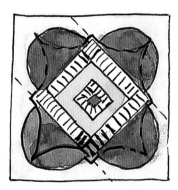

Make eighty B blocks (apricot-colored background) the same way you made the A blocks.

Sew the petals down. To keep the petals lying flat, fasten them by using a curved sewing line, which each time leads from the corner to the middle of the semicircle (as illustrated). Use bright-red sewing thread.

> **TIP for Longarm Quilting**
> Wait to sew the petals down until the pieced-together quilt is stretched out on the machine, then you can do this work more comfortably.

Trim the Blocks

Use the square ruler to trim all the blocks to exactly 5½" × 5½" (14 × 14 cm). Sew more flowers than absolutely necessary so that you can exchange individual colors.

Piecing the Quilt Together
(Lesson 9)

Arrange the blocks so they are "standing" on a tip. Start with seven B blocks (apricot-colored background) and place five A blocks (white background) in the gaps underneath. Arrange eleven B block rows, one below the other, with the bottom row consisting of B blocks. Put the A blocks in the spaces in between. Distribute colors at random.

For the edge triangles, cut eight squares of 10¼" × 10¼" (26 × 26 cm) and divide each of them twice diagonally into four triangles, with the grain running along the long edge. Insert the edge triangles. For the triangles at the corners, divide two squares of 5½" × 5½" (14 × 14 cm) once along the bias. Piece the quilt top together in diagonal rows.

Quilting
(Lessons 11 and 12)

Assemble the backing, volume fleece, and quilt top one atop the other. Using natural-white yarn, quilt along the block seams, and quilt a small four-petaled flower on each seam intersection, by hand or by machine. Work a pretty bow pattern on the border triangles.

Binding
(Lesson 13)

Bind the basted edge with a medium-green bias binding.

Arrange the blocks diagonally, starting with A blocks, then add the border and corner triangles.

Quilting suggestion.

Shadow Frames (Flying Frames)
1½ × 1⅛ yards (127 × 100 cm)

Cut it out! How fitting is the title of the book the graffiti child is reading in the photo.

▥ Materials
Fabric
- ⅓ yard (0.30 m) vividly striped fabric for the frames.
- 1 yard (0.90 m) dark blue for the shadows.
- 2¼ yards (2.00 m) sky blue (here hand-dyed) for the background and the border triangles.

Other
- 1⅔ × 1⅓ yards (150 × 120 cm) backing fabric.
- 1⅔ × 1⅓ yards (150 × 120 cm) volume fleece.
- sky-blue quilting thread.
- 12′ (360 cm) dark-blue diagonal strips.

▥ Instructions
Cutting Out
(Lesson 1: Basic Shapes)
Cut dark-blue strips about ¾" (2 cm) wide (inner shadow) and 3¼" (8 cm) wide (outer shadow). In addition, you need ¾"-wide (2 cm) sky-blue strips. Piece one wide dark-blue and a narrow sky-blue strip together along the lengthwise edge. Iron the seam allowance to the dark fabric. Cut out units of about 1¼" (3 cm) wide from these pieced-together strips. These will be the outer shadows.

For the final round, cut out sky-blue strips of 4" (10 cm) wide. For the border triangles, you need three sky-blue squares of 11" × 11" (28 × 28 cm) divided twice along the bias. This yields sixteen triangles, with the straight grain running along the long edge. For the four corners, cut out two sky-blue squares of 7⅞" × 7⅞" (20 × 20 cm) and divide them once along the bias.

Use a ruler to cut them out, but you do not need to measure accurately to the millimeter.

32 Shadow Frames
(Lesson 4: Log Cabin)
For the block center squares, you need thirty-two squares of 1½" × 1½" (4 × 4 cm) in sky blue.

1st round (half): For the inner shadows, sew a 1¼"-wide (3 cm) dark-blue strip to two adjoining edges of the center square. This is only a half log cabin round and is thus finished.

2nd round: Now attach the frame fabric. Cut the frame fabric into strips, with the pattern running crosswise across the cut strips. Vary the widths from ¾–1½" (2–4 cm), and cut at a slight angle. Sew the frame fabric on to all four edges of the center unit.

1st round (half): Sew shadow strips (¾" [2 cm]) onto two edges of the center square (2" × 2" [5 × 5 cm]).

2nd round: Sew on the striped frame fabrics (1¼–2" [3–5 cm] wide).

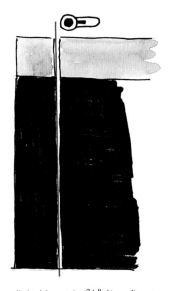

Sew a light-blue strip (¾" [2 cm]) onto a dark-blue strip (3¼" [8 cm]). From this, cut out units about 1¼" (3 cm) wide.

3rd round (half): Sew one each of the 4"-wide (10 cm), dark-blue strips, and of the 1"-wide (2.5 cm), sky-blue strips on to the lengthwise edges. Iron the seam allowance to the dark fabric. Cut sixty-four units of about 1½" (4 cm) wide from these pieced-together strips. Sew one each of these units to the two edges of the block, where there is no inner shadow. The dark-blue fabrics should meet at the corner, with the sky-blue corners diagonally across from each other. Cut off the protruding ends as necessary. Again, this is only a half round.

4th round: Next comes the background, which is added as the fourth round of sky-blue strips, about 4" (10 cm) wide.

Sew 32 Blocks

Using a square ruler, cut all the blocks to a uniform size; here, it is exactly 7⅞" × 7⅞" (20 × 20 cm).

Piecing the Quilt Together
(Lesson 9)

Arrange the blocks so they are "standing" on a tip. Lay out five rows of four blocks each, and each time arrange three blocks in the gaps. Make sure that all the shadows are facing downward. Add on the border triangles and four corner triangles. Piece the blocks together for the quilt top.

3rd round (half): Sew the shadow units to both edges of the center unit that lie opposite to the inner shadow. Cut off the protruding ends each time.

4th round: Sky-blue strips (4" [10 cm]).

Quilting
(Lessons 11 and 12)

Assemble the backing, volume fleece, and quilt top one atop the other. Quilt an oval feather pattern with light-blue thread (with the longarm) or an orange peel pattern (by hand) along the block seams.

Binding
(Lesson 13)

Round off the corners of the quilt using a plate or compass and baste once around the entire edge. Bind the quilt with dark-blue bias binding.

Arrangement of the blocks,

quilting suggestion,
shaping the corners.

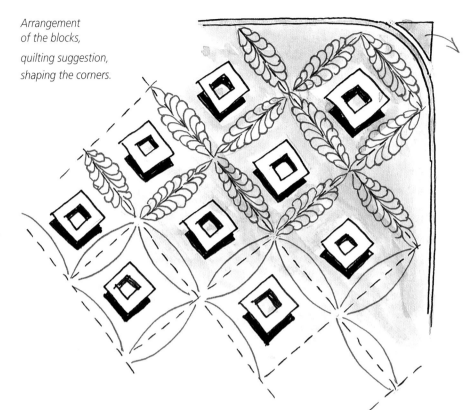

Seersucker Log Cabin
2½ × 1¾ yards (224 × 160 cm)

Seersucker fabric can be surprisingly easy to sew with; you should just avoid ironing it. Here we have used a set of white bed linen, but you can always work with "normal" cotton fabrics, and of course with other colors.

▥ Materials
Fabric
- Fabric pack with about ninety assorted colors, at least 2¾" × 2¾" (7 × 7 cm), for the center squares.
- 1¼ yards (1.10 m) striped fabric, white with dark blue (or black and white), stripe width about ¾" (5 mm), for round 1.

- A set of seersucker bed linen, solid, two colors, here light blue and dark blue; it must be prewashed for rounds 2 and 3.
- ⅞ yard (0.70 m) copper red solid or slightly patterned for the border strips.

Or alternatively for the centers:
- Four pieces of ombre fabrics, light to dark: 6" (15 cm) each in red, yellow, blue, and green.
- ⅝ yard (0.50 m) rainbow cloth, all colors.

Or alternatively, use instead of the seersucker fabric:
- 5½ yards (5.00 m) light blue and 5½ yards (5.00 m) dark blue, solid or slightly patterned.

Other
- A heavy book.
- 2⅝ × 2 yards (240 × 180 cm) backing fabric.
- 2⅝ × 2 yards (240 × 180 cm) volume fleece
- Light-blue quilting thread.
- 25½" (780 cm) dark blue bias binding.

▥ Instructions
Cutting Out
(Lesson 1: Basic Shapes)
For the block centers, cut out eighty-eight squares about 2¾" × 2¾" (7 × 7 cm) from the rainbow colors. Cut the blue-and-white or black-and-white-striped fabric into strips about 1¼" (3 cm) wide, and the seersucker fabric into strips of about 2" (5 cm) wide, each time in light blue and dark blue. Use a ruler to cut them out, but you do not need to measure accurately to the millimeter. Cut the seersucker strips across the direction of the stripes and work sparingly, because you could run out of fabric.

88 Log Cabin Blocks
(Lesson 4: Log Cabin)

1st round: Sew a black-and-white-striped strip to all four sides of the center square. Iron the seam allowance to the outside.

Choose forty-four units with light-colored centers (A blocks) and forty-four with dark centers (B blocks). Intermediate shades fit into both groups and make the distribution easier.

2nd round: Attach a dark-blue (forty-four A blocks) seersucker strip to each of the light center blocks and a light-blue one (forty-four B blocks) around the dark center blocks. Since you should not iron seersucker fabric, smooth out the blocks with your palms. Then stack them together and weigh them down overnight with a thick book.

Next, use a square ruler to trim all the blocks to exactly 6" × 6" (15 × 15 cm). Then position the square ruler on the fabric so that it is slanted to the right on the light blocks and slanted to the left on the dark blocks. This gives the blocks the irregular quality you want.

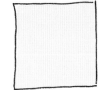

Center squares (2¾" × 2¾" [7 × 7 cm]).

1st round: Sew the striped fabric around the center square.

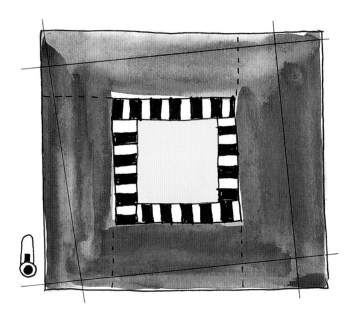

2nd round A block: Sew light-blue fabric around the center unit. Place a square ruler slanted to the left, and cut out the block exactly (here 6" × 6" (15 × 15 cm]).

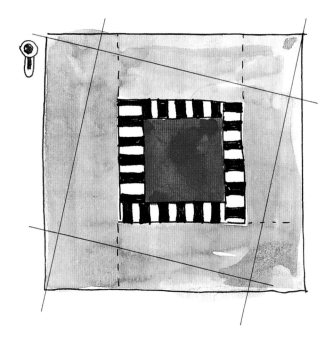

2nd round B block: Sew dark-blue fabric around the center unit. Place the square ruler slanted to the right, and cut out the block exactly (here 6" × 6" (15 × 15 cm]).

3rd round A block: Sew light-blue fabric around the dark edges.

3rd round B block: Sew dark-blue fabric around the light edges.

3rd round: Sew a dark-blue seersucker strip around each of the light-blue edges (forty-four B blocks) and a light-blue strip around each of the dark-blue ones (forty-four A blocks). Weigh the blocks down again with a thick book to flatten them. Later, trim all the blocks to the same size; here it is exactly 8¼" × 8¼" (21 × 21 cm).

> **TIP**
> If you do not have enough seersucker fabric, sew individual rounds of "normal" cotton fabric. In our project, we even unstitched the button placket on the bed linen so that we had enough fabric.

Piecing the Quilt Together
(Lesson 9)
Arrange the blocks in eleven horizontal rows of eight blocks each. Start with an A block in the upper-left corner and arrange the other blocks in an alternating pattern. Distribute the colors of the block centers randomly. Piece the blocks together into the quilt top. It is practical that the seersucker fabric is stretchable, because all the seam intersections come together easily.

> **TIP**
> If you really want to iron the quilt top, iron dry, without dampening the fabric. Lay each seam over the edge of the ironing board and only iron along here.

Borders
(Lesson 10)
Copper red, 3¼" (8 cm) cutting width, straight corners.

Quilting
(Lessons 11 and 12)
Assemble the backing, volume fleece, and quilt top one atop the other. Use light blue thread to quilt by hand or machine in the seams of the light blue fabric and once in the quilt border seam.

Binding
(Lesson 13)
Bind the basted edge with dark-blue bias binding.

REVERSE APPLIQUE TECHNIQUE AND OPEN EDGES

Lesson 7:
Reverse Applique Technique
Projects: Diver's Paradise, Millefleur, Colored Saucers

Called reverse applique technique in the United States, this technique is sometimes called "piping technique" and is also known as "Mola"; it is done using a machine. You need the fabric for the block (background), a contrasting reverse applique, and the fabric that you place behind or underneath. The reverse applique technique works well for open or closed shapes.

Place the reverse applique fabric, right sides facing, on the background fabric. Draw the shape on the reverse applique fabric (here, a circle). Sew all around on the line. Inside the shape, cut out both layers of fabric up to seam allowance width. Notch the seam allowance at short intervals close up to the seam. Pull the reverse applique fabric through the opening to the back.

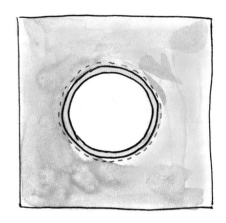

Flatten the opening edge with your fingernail. At the same time, let about 1 mm of the reverse applique fabric show through. If needed, baste one time around the opening. Finally, insert the selected fabric behind the opening and, using normal thread, sew around the opening close to the edge. Cut back any protruding fabric on the wrong side up to the seam allowance width.

Openings in Reverse Applique Technique

Place the reverse applique fabric, right sides facing, on the block. Draw the desired shape (e.g., a fish, a circle) on the reverse applique fabric and sew along the drawn line.

Cut out both layers of fabric within the shape, up to 3–4 mm from the seam. Notch the seam allowance with sharp small scissors, close up to the seam. Pull the reverse applique fabric through the opening to the back. Iron the opening, or smooth out the edge with your fingernail. It looks very nice if 1 mm of reverse applique fabric remains visible.

Now place the fabric for the shape (such as colorful for a fish or pastel for a flower center) behind the opening and fasten it with pins. On the front side, sew close to the edge around the opening. For this, use ordinary thread in the color of the quilt top and do not sew on the edge, which appears as piping. Finally, on the wrong side, trim off the protruding edges of the piping and the fabric underneath.

Open Edges
Projects: Denim Blossoms, Serenade
If you use fabrics that do not fray at the edge, such as denim, thick wool, felted knitted wool, loden, or fiber fleece, you do not need to use the reverse applique technique. Cut the desired shape directly out of the fabric and line the opening with a new fabric. Either fasten on this fabric by hand using running stitches or sew around the opening with the sewing machine. Cut back any excess fabric edges on the wrong side, up to the seam allowance width.

Lesson 8:
Freehand Embroidery with a Sewing Machine
Projects: Strange Birds, Bird Cushions, Millefleur

Freehand embroidery resembles free-motion machine quilting, except that here you do not sew through all three layers of the quilt. To reinforce the fabric, you should iron thin volume fleece to the wrong side. Lining with adhesive fleece does indeed reinforce the fabric, but it is tedious to remove it from the wrong side. Work with a contrasting color thread so that the embroidery is displayed to advantage. Practice first on a sample piece.

Sewing Machine Embroidery Frame
Many sewing machines have an embroidery frame (unfortunately relatively small). Place the outer ring on the work surface and spread the fabric right side up over it. Now put on the inner ring and press it firmly into the outer ring. The fabric lies on the table surface and not on top of the embroidery ring, as you are used to for hand embroidery.

Setting Up a Sewing Machine
Insert the darning foot into the sewing machine. Lower the fabric mover and/or adjust the pressure of the needle bar to 0. Use the same thread for upper and lower and if necessary loosen the needle thread tension a little. Set the stitch straight. The stitch length setting does not matter.

Embroidering
Slide the embroidery ring under the sewing machine foot. Lower the presser foot (this is important because of the thread tension). For some machine types the foot should be half lowered. Now press down the foot pedal steadily and guide the embroidery ring in the desired direction.

Embroidering without a Ring
Using both hands lying to the right and left of the needle, slide the fabric through under the sewing machine.

Motifs
Roughly sketch your desired motif, set an outline or a guide line, or work completely freehand, without presketching. With practice, the stitches will be of the same length and your motions even. Lockstitch the thread at the beginning and end of the stitching line with a few stitches on the spot, or draw it to the back of the quilt and knot it there.

> **TIP**
> You can just glue the fabric and draw the legs and flourishes with a textile pen, thus saving having to do machine embroidery. But beware: you can never wash the pillow.

Longarm Quilting
Anyone who works on a longarm quilting machine waits to embroider the lines until the sewing or gluing on the quilt top is finished. Then assemble the top, fleece, and backing as usual. Use a contrasting-colored thread and quilt through all the layers. This is embroidering and quilting at the same time and saves one work step.

Denim Blossoms
2⅜ × 2⅛ yards (217 × 190 cm)

This cheerfully colorful quilt turns any old sofa into an ornamental piece. Depending on your personal supply of denim, you have to cut up jeans that are more or less light and dark. You will have to change the arrangement accordingly. Stay flexible. The groups of four denim blossoms also work well with the "quilt-as-you-go" method, in which the blocks, together with the backing and volume fleece, are sewn and quilted until finished, one at a time. The sections are then pieced together with sashings.

■ Materials
Fabric
- Ten to eleven old pairs of jeans (20–25 squares per pair of jeans).
- ⅔ yard (0.60 m) bright yellow for the A blocks.
- ⅔ yard (0.60 m) colorful, large-patterned fabric for the A blocks.
- ⅔ yard (0.60 m) bright turquoise for the B blocks.
- 1 yard (0.90 m) turquoise-green, large-patterned fabric for the B blocks.
- ⅔ yard (0.60 m) bright green for the C blocks.
- ⅔ yard (0.60 m) hot-pink large-patterned fabric for the C blocks.
- ⅓ yard (0.25 m) light blue, solid (such as light jeans) for the sashings between the A blocks.
- ⅓ yard (0.25 m) dark blue-green, solid (like dark jeans) for the sashings between the B blocks and around them.
- ⅓ yard (0.25 m) medium blue, solid (such as medium jeans) for the sashings between the C blocks.
- ¼ yard (0.20 m) black-and-white striped (stripe width of about ⅓" [1 cm]) for the accent stripe around the middle section (A blocks) and for the binding.

Other
- Checkered paper.
- Stiff cardboard.
- Heat-sensitive or water-soluble pen.
- Small curved scissors.
- Small fabric scissors.
- 2⅝ × 2⅓ yards (230 × 210 cm) backing fabric.
- 2⅝ × 2⅓ yards (230 × 210 cm) volume fleece.
- Blue sewing and quilting thread.

■ Instructions
224 Denim Squares
Cut off the seams, pockets, hems, and waistbands from the jeans. Make a 6" × 6" (15 × 15 cm) pattern from the stiff cardboard. Using the pattern, draw squares on the pieces of denim and cut them out with scissors. You need 224 denim squares of 6" × 6" (15 × 15 cm).

Cutting Out the Blossom Shapes
Make a blossom pattern from stiff paper. For this, fold a sheet of checkered paper twice lengthwise and crosswise, and draw a quarter of the blossom on it (see illustration). Cut along the edge of the blossom and unfold the blossom. Glue the blossom to stiff cardboard and cut it out. This is your pattern.

Transfer the blossom shape to the center of the wrong side of the denim squares and cut it out carefully along the lines, so that the blossom remains intact.

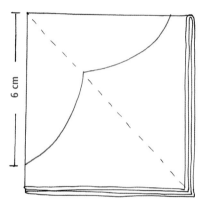

Make a blossom pattern of folded paper, paste it to cardboard, and cut it out.

Cut blossom shapes from each denim square.

Lay aside the cut-out blossom.

224 Half-Square Triangles

Calculation: A 6"-wide (15 cm) strip, cut selvedge to selvedge, yields six squares of 6" × 6" (15 × 15 cm).

Cut out squares of about 6" × 6" (15 × 15 cm) from the cotton fabrics. Use the convenient width of a quilt ruler to do this. You need for the blocks:

- A blocks: twenty-four yellow and twenty-four multicolored squares.
- B blocks: thirty-six turquoise and thirty-six blue multicolored squares.
- C blocks: fifty-two green and fifty-two red multicolored squares.

Place one multicolored and one solid square each together, right sides facing, and divide both on the bias, either freehand or using a ruler. Leave the resulting triangles one atop the other. Sew them together along the bias edge. Each time you get two, two-color squares (half-square triangle). Press the seam allowance to the multicolored fabric.

Sew

- forty-eight multicolored/yellow
- seventy-two multicolored/turquoise
- 104 multicolored/green half-square triangles.

Denim Blossoms

Place a two-color square on the work surface, right side up, and spread a denim square, with the blossom shape cut out, on top. Align the seam so that it runs right to two diagonally opposite corners of the blossom shape. Insert a pin through both layers of fabric at each corner. Set the sewing machine to a very short stitch and use the lower needle

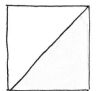

a) 48 multicolored/yellow half-square triangles (for A blocks).

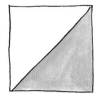

b) 72 multicolored/ turquoise half-square triangles (for B blocks).

c) 104 multicolored/ green half-square triangles (for C blocks).

position (if there is one). Use blue thread to sew once around the blossom shape. Start on the side of a petal, at seam allowance width distance, and sew all the way into the inner tip. Leave the needle in the fabric at this point, raise the presser foot, and turn the block. Sew to the tip on the other side of the petal, and here widen the distance from the edge back to seam allowance width.

On the wrong side, trim the colored cotton fabric back to ⅓" (1 cm) from the seam.

Sew

- 48 A blossoms with multicolored/ bright yellow centers in the light denim squares.
- 72 B blossoms with blue turquoise centers in the dark denim squares.
- 104 C blossoms with red-green centers in medium denim squares

Forty-eight A denim blossoms.

Seventy-two B denim blossoms.

104 C denim blossoms.

Example: View of the wrong side of A denim blossom.

Four-Patch Blocks
(Lesson 9: Piecing the Quilt Together)
Piece four same-color denim blossoms together. The color of the denim should be similar and the inside color the same (thus, four multicolored/yellow or four red/yellow blossoms). Place the blossoms so that the color faces toward the middle. Sew the upper pair and the lower pair, right sides facing. Do not cut off the thread in between, but take the work off the machine. On the wrong side, press the seam allowances open. Then stitch along both sides of the seam, close to the edge on the right side of the fabric. Then join the cross seam and, as you do so, press the seam allowances open and stitch close along the edge on the right side of the fabric. This lets all the seams lie flat. If necessary, trim all the blocks to the same size; here it is exactly 11½" × 11½" (29 × 29 cm).

Sew
- 12 four-patch blocks of the A blossoms
- 18 four-patch blocks of the B blossoms
- 26 four-patch blocks of the C blossoms

TIP
If you use the "quilt-as-you-go" method, now make each four-patch block individually and quilt it finished with volume fleece and backing. Sew around the outer edges with long stitches, so that the fabric layers do not slip out of place at the border. Piece the blocks together with sashings. Neaten the open seams on the wrong side with more sashings that you sew on by hand.

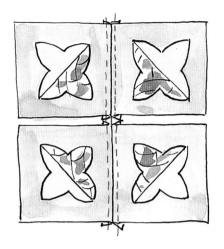

Sample four-patch A block: Piece together four A denim blossoms, the colored triangles pointing toward the center. First, sew together the adjacent denim blossoms. Press the seam allowances open. Stitch along the right and left of the seam, close to the edge.

Sample four-patch A block: Then join the cross seam, press apart the seam allowances, and likewise stitch along the right and left close to the edge.

TIP
The arrangement and grouping of the blocks depends on your range of denim. Change the arrangement, depending on whether you have more or less of light and dark denim.

Sewing Plan

Arrange the blocks on a sufficiently large surface. Here, we have framed a light central part with a series of dark four-patch blocks and added an outer border of 7×8 four-patch blocks in intermediate shades of color.

Sashings

Piece together the four-patch blocks with sashings. Avoid making very thick seams and seam intersections. Cut the sashings to exactly 1¼" (3 cm) wide and select dark strips for the dark blocks, medium for medium, and light for the lighter blocks.

Piecing the Quilt Together

Start with the middle section and piece together the A blocks with medium blue sashings. Sew black-and-white-striped strips that are exactly 1¼" (3 cm) wide around the finished middle section. Then sew the two outer rounds, using sashings of matching colors, in appropriately long rows. Attach them each time to the right and left, then top and bottom.

Quilting

(Lessons 11 and 12)

Quilt in the seams around the four-patch blocks by hand or with a sewing machine. With the longarm quilting machine, repeat the blossom shape like an echo, which extends 3–4 mm beyond the sewing line and again runs back up to the tip.

Binding

(Lesson 13)

Bind the quilt with a black-and-white-striped, straight-cut, double-layer fabric, with a cutting width of 2⅓" (6 cm).

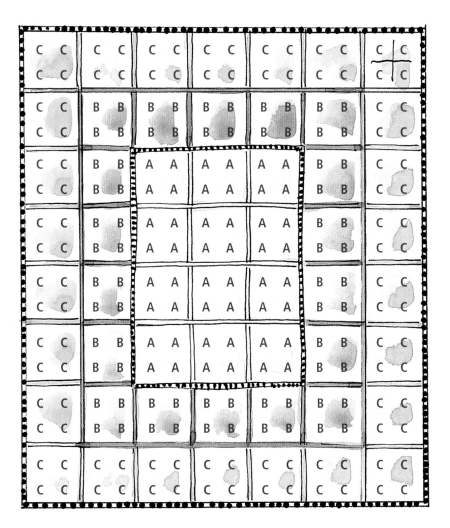

Sewing plan: Sew together the four-patch groups with sashings.

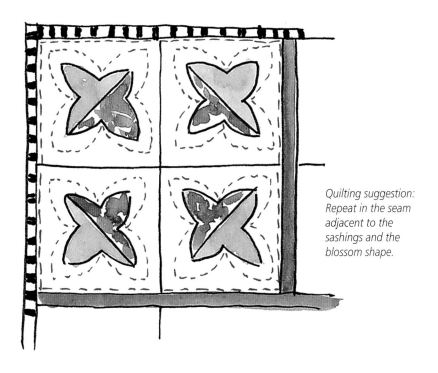

Quilting suggestion: Repeat in the seam adjacent to the sashings and the blossom shape.

Millefleur
2½ × 2⅜ yards (228 × 215 cm)

The flowers are sewn in reverse applique technique and freehand embroidery. Keep the background light in color and the flower centers in pastel colors, so that the sketchy embroidery will look to good advantage. The straight stem and the always-similar leaf shape create the ordering element. In the visual arts, pastel colors are considered those to which enough white was added so that they are refracted and light. Their effect is powdery, soft, and gentle. Pastel colors lend a room elegance and lightness.

▦ Materials
Fabric
- 1⅔ yards (1.50 m) total amount of different pastel colors, solid, for the flower centers.
- 7⅔ yards (7.00 m) muslin (1⅔ yards [150 cm] wide), natural white, prewashed, for the background.
- 1⅔ yards (1.50 m) white (thin quality) for the reverse applique.
- ⅔ yard (0.60 m) light blue and white striped for the binding,

Or alternatively for the flower centers:
- Sample books, 360 pieces of fabric, at least 2" × 2" (5 × 5 cm) large; use only light fabrics, but no white or natural white.
- About twenty pastel-colored, pre-cut strips, 2½" (6.5 cm) wide.

Other
- Hard pencil or marker.
- Sharp-pointed scissors.
- If needed, 1⅛ yards (1.00 m) thin, iron-on volume fleece.
- If needed, a large embroidery hoop for a sewing machine.

- Embroidery foot (darning foot/freehand quilting foot) for a sewing machine.
- Dark-gray sewing thread for embroidery.
- 2¾ × 2⅝ yards (250 × 230 cm) backing fabric.
- 2¾ × 2⅝ yards (250 × 230 cm) volume fleece.
- Natural-white quilting thread.

▦ Instructions
Cutting Out
(Lesson 1: Basic Shapes)
Cut the muslin into strips about 4" (10 cm) wide. Separate out a total of at least 360 pieces of different lengths, from 6" to 12" (15 to 30 cm), so that the petals will be of different sizes. You also need 360 white 3¼" × 3¼" (8 × 8 cm) squares for reverse applique and 360 pastel colored squares, approximately 2" × 2" (5 × 5 cm), for the flower centers.

> **Note**
> I got the measurement for the narrow, long blocks from some strips of fabric I bought very cheaply from a bed linen factory a long time ago. It could be more convenient for you to work with wider strips, then sew correspondingly fewer A blocks, and possibly larger flowers.

About 360 Flower Centers

(Lesson 7: Reverse Applique Technique)

Lay a white square on the upper third of a muslin strip and draw the flower center with a hard pencil. The flower centers should be ¾–1¼" (2–3 cm) in size. Draw the shapes of a circle, oval, thimble shape, and a slanting oval on the reverse applique fabric. Sew using a short stitch length (e.g., stitch length 1.5) all around the line. Cut out both layers of fabric within the shape, up to 3–4 mm from the seam. Notch the seam allowance with a small, sharp pair of scissors up to the seam, and pull the reverse applique fabric through the hole toward the wrong side. Iron the opening.

TIP
When sewing small circles and ovals, set your machine to "needle down position," "half speed," and work without the top fabric mover. Always raise the presser foot so you can turn the fabric easily.

Pin a 2" × 2" (5 × 5 cm) pastel square behind the opening and stitch all around on the right side with a medium stitch length (e.g., stitch length of 2.5), close to the edge. Now trim back the protruding fabric on the wrong side: the pastels down to about 3 mm, and the white reverse applique fabric to approximately 5 mm from the seam. This prevents the reverse applique fabric from showing through the light background fabric.

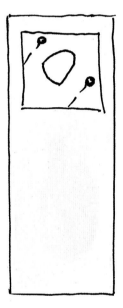

Place the reverse applique fabric, right sides facing, on the block fabric. Draw on the flower center shape. Sew all around directly on the drawn line.

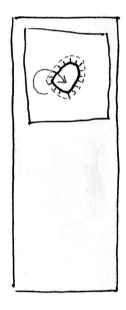

Cut out both layers in the middle. Notch the seam allowances. Pull the reverse applique fabric through the hole to the back.

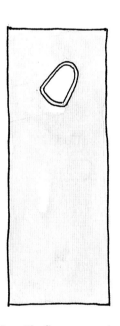

Iron. The flower center is now a neat opening.

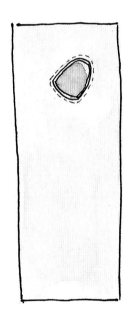

Put the pastel colored flower fabric beneath the opening. Stitch close to the edge around the opening.

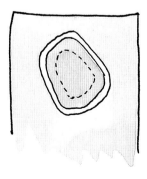

On the wrong side cut back the protruding fabric and cut the colored fabric back closer to the seam than the white reverse applique fabric.

Different shapes for the flower centers (round, oval, and thimble-shaped).

TIP
Definitely sew some extra flowers so you can exchange them and fill in any gaps.

About 360 Flower Blocks
(Lesson 8: Freehand Embroidery)

Fashion the flowers in freehand embroidery technique using anthracite-colored thread. To prepare the fabric for freehand embroidery, you can iron thin volume fleece to the wrong side of the block. This makes it more stable and easier to work with. Use a sewing machine to "draw" the petals around the colored center, and a stem with small leaves underneath. Sew each line twice, so that it stands out clearly. The two lines do not have to run exactly one over the other; this emphasizes the sketchy quality. Start a few millimeters below the flower at the X. Starting from there, embroider the flower to the right and left and all around (twice), then stitch the stem downward and embroider the leaves (twice) to the left and right of the stem, and back up to the starting point X. Do not make the flowers any closer than ¾" (2 cm) to the edge of the block.

If you like, embroider a few flying insects in the open areas above the flowers.

TIP for Longarm Quilting
First cut out all the blocks to 3¼" (8 cm) wide and in varying lengths (as described below). It is not necessary to iron fleece on as a lining. Sew the entire quilt top finished and embroider/quilt the flowers with a longarm machine directly through the three layers of the quilt.

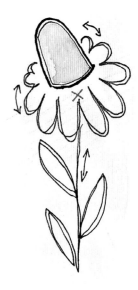

Round center: Start the petals at the X. Sew around the flowers twice. From the X, stitch the stems going downward. From the bottom to top, sew each leaf twice to the right and left of the stem, then back up to the X.

Thimble-shaped center: Start the petals at X, embroider toward the side, and let the petals get smaller, then back to the X. Do this next on the other side (just as before), and again back to the X. From the X, stitch the stems going downward. From the bottom to top, sew each leaf twice to the right and left of the stem, then back up to the X.

Oval center: At the X, start with large petals that get smaller toward the side, and stitch very small petals on the opposite side that get a bit larger toward the other side, then large petals again back to the X. Stitch the entire pattern twice. From the X, stitch the stems going downward. From the bottom to top, sew each leaf twice to the right and left of the stem, then back up to the X.

Quilting or embroidery suggestion for a small insect.

Now trim the flower blocks to an equal width. Here it is 3¼" (8 cm), a measurement that resulted from the strips that I had. The height of the blocks is between 6" and 12" (15 and 30 cm).

Prepare some strips of muslin of the same width to fill in any gaps at the top and bottom edges of the quilt top.

Piecing the Quilt Together
(Lesson 9)
The quilt is pieced together of thirty-six longitudinal rows. Sew nine to eleven blocks, each time one beneath the other, until it reaches about 3⅝ yards (230 cm) long. Offset the blocks so that the flowers are distributed irregularly. To do this, make some blocks shorter if necessary. Fill in the gaps at the top and bottom edges of the quilt with muslin. Before quilting, the quilt shown here is 2½ yards (220 cm) wide.

Quilting
(Lessons 11 and 12)
Quilt by hand or with a sewing machine along the lengthwise seams between the rows of blocks.

Binding
(Lesson 13)
Bind the quilt with a light-blue-striped, straight-cut, double-layer strip of fabric with a cutting width of 2⅓" (6 cm).

Millefleur Child's Quilt
1⅓ × 1⅛ yards (120 × 100 cm)

With its ninety flowers, this child's bed cover is just as charming and effective as the large "Millefleur" quilt (pgs. 99–103). When doing the machine embroidery for the stems and leaves, you do not have to run the lines exactly one atop the other. This maintains the sketchy quality of the work.

■ Materials
Fabric
- ½ yard (0.40 m) total amount of different pastel colors, solid or slightly patterned.
- 2¼ yards (2.00 m) muslin (1⅔ yards [150 cm] wide), natural white, prewashed, for the background.
- 1⅔ yards (1.50 m) white (thin quality) for the reverse applique.
- ⅓ yard (0.30 m) pink-and-white-striped fabric for the binding.

Other
- Hard pencil or marker.
- Sharp-pointed scissors.
- If needed, 1⅛ yards (1.00 m) thin, iron-on volume fleece.
- If needed, a large embroidery frame for the sewing machine.
- Embroidery foot (darning foot/ freehand quilting foot) for the sewing machine.
- 1⅝ × 1⅓ yards (140 × 120 cm) backing fabric.
- 1⅝ × 1⅓ yards (140 × 120 cm) volume fleece.
- Dark-blue yarn for embroidery

■ Instructions
Use the instructions for the large quilt as your guide. Sew ninety flowers as described there. Sew eighteen lengthwise rows of five to six flowers each. Adjust the block lengths so that you get a common length. Join the lengthwise rows together. Assemble the layers and quilt (see large quilt).

Binding
(Lesson 13)
Bind the quilt with a pink-and-white-striped, straight-cut, double-layer strip of fabric, with a cutting width of 2⅓" (6 cm).

Diver's Paradise
2¼ × 2¾ yards (200 × 250 cm)

Some quilters have specialized in dyeing fabrics and sell these fabrics. A large piece of cloth, dyed in rainbow colors, was the inspiration for this quilt. It is reminiscent of the "Coral Reef" from my book *Water Patchwork* but is not as complicated to sew.

■ Materials
Fabric
- Sheets of 2¼ × 2¾ yards (200 × 250 cm), dyed in rainbow colors.
- 4⅜ yards (4.00 m) black for the piping around the fish.
- ¼–⅓ yard (0.25–0.30 m) each of approximately twelve different vibrantly colored fabrics, rich in contrast, strikingly dotted and striped, in all colors, for the fish.

Other
- Chalk.
- Stencil cardboard to make the fish shapes.
- 2½ × 3 yards (220 × 270 cm) backing fabric.
- 2½ × 3 yards (220 × 270 cm) polyester fleece.
- Rainbow-colored hand or machine quilting thread.
- 10⅛ yards (9.20 m) black-satin bias binding, extra wide, for the binding.

■ Instructions
Fish Patterns
Browse through picture books and the Internet for fish motifs. Choose pictures that show an entire fish from the side view. Trace the contours and then enlarge these pictures to the required format. Round off the tips and flatten out any deep indentations. The smallest fish shown here are about 2⅓" (6 cm) high and 4¾" (12 cm) long, and the largest are about 10" (25 cm) high and 13¾" (35 cm) long.

75 Fish
(Lesson 7: Reverse Applique Technique)
The colorful fish are worked using the reverse applique technique. Cut out black rectangles, each around 2" (5 cm) bigger than the planned fish. Allow at least 4" (10 cm) open up to the quilt edge and group small fish into shoals. Do not set the fish any closer than 2–2⅓" (5–6 cm) apart.

Work fish by fish. Pin the reverse applique fabric, right sides facing, onto the rainbow fabric. Use chalk to draw a fish shape on the reverse applique fabric. To do this, make several different fish shapes out of cardboard to use as outlines. Sew around the contours and cut out the inner fish shape through both layers of fabric. Trim to a seam allowance about ⅓" (1 cm) wide on the seam. Notch the seam allowance all around up to the seam, being especially careful in the corners of the tail fin and of the tip of the head. Pull the reverse applique fabric through the hole to the back and press the edges smooth. Leave about 1 mm of showing through as piping. Baste by hand once around the fish shape.

Black

Background

Lay the black reverse applique fabric, right sides facing, on the "water surface" and trace the fish outline. Sew along the line. Cut out the inner shape. Notch the seam allowances. Push the reverse applique fabric through the opening to the back. Press the edge smooth and let 1 mm of reverse applique show through as piping. Hand baste around the opening.

Place the vividly patterned fabric behind the opening. Make shoals and groups of matching colors. From the right side, quilt close to the edge using thread the same color as the water surface. Remove the basting threads. Trim away any protruding fabric on the wrong side to the seam allowance width. After assembling the layers, quilt aquatic plants on the top.

Place some spotted or vividly striped fabrics behind the openings. Use the same color to make the fish for any one group. Baste or pin the fish fabric firmly around the opening. Quilt with matching-color thread close to the edge around the shape and remove any basting threads. Trim any protruding reverse applique fabric on the wrong side and trim the multicolored fish fabric up to the seam allowance width.

Arrangement

When arranging and distributing the fish, follow the photograph or find your an arrangement that you like.

Quilting

(Lessons 11 and 12)

Assemble the backing, volume fleece, and quilt top one atop the other. Use matching multicolor quilting thread to quilt the growing aquatic plants. Quilt close up to the fish, but leave the fish themselves untouched.

Binding

(Lesson 13)

Bind the quilt edge with a wide black-satin bias binding.

Shadow Fish
2⅓ × 1¼ yards (213 × 104 cm)

The black shadows lend the fish a very graphic effect. Use fabric in shades of rainbow colors to cut out the multicolored fish, or use the same fish as in the "Diver's Paradise" quilt. The top layer of tulle makes the quilt a bit scratchy, but that is no problem for a wall quilt.

▥ Materials
Fabric
- 1⅔ yards (1.50 m) rainbow-colored ombre fabric for the fish.
- 1⅔ yards (1.50 m) black, solid, for the shadows.
- 2½ yards (2.20 m) very bright turquoise for the background.
- 2½ yards (2.20 m) blue tulle for the top.

Other
- Finest-grade tailor pins (no glass head pins or the like).
- 2⅝ × 1⅓ yards (240 × 120 cm) backing fabric.
- 2⅝ × 1⅓ yards (240 × 120 cm) volume fleece.
- Light-blue hand or machine quilting thread.
- 5¾ yards (520 cm) medium-blue bias binding for the binding.

▥ Instructions
Fish Patterns
Look for fish motifs as described for the "Diver's Paradise" quilt (pg. 106).

75 Fish
Lay the black fabric and rainbow ombre fabric one atop the other, both right side up. Iron over the surfaces, which will then adhere lightly to each other. Use a suitable marker to draw the fish shapes close together and without a seam allowance on the multicolored fabric. Insert a pin through each fish. Cut out both layers at the same time. Lay aside the fish for each color and/or shape group together.

Lay the rainbow fabric on the black fabric. Cut out the fish from two layers of fabric at the same time.

Slide the fabric to the side a bit, so that the black fabric creates the effect of a shadow. All the shadows must face the same direction.

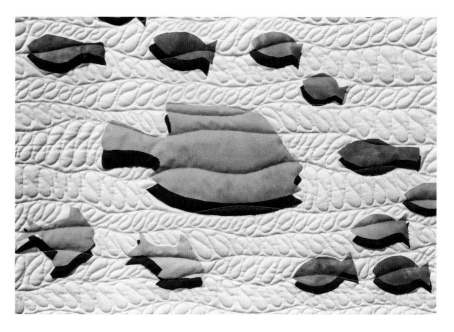

Arrangement

Follow the illustration or find your own arrangement that you like.

Fasten the background fabric lengthways on your design wall. Pin on the fish and their shadows. Slide each shadow downward by about ⅓–¾" (1–2 cm). Group fish with the same contours, sizes, and colors together. Change the fishes' swimming direction and tilt the bodies upward or downward. If you like, cut out some circles to make bubbles, also with black shadows. To pin on the fish, be sure to use fine tailor's pins without a glass or plastic head.

Spread the tulle over the quilt top and fasten it firmly with plenty of pins. First sew flat, wavy lines about 2–3¼" (5–8 cm) apart across the surface. As you are doing this, change the sewing direction for each line. This holds the fish fast between the background fabric and the tulle, so that they cannot slip down. Remove the pins through the fine netting of the tulle.

Quilting

(Lessons 11 and 12)

Assemble the backing, volume fleece, and quilt top one atop the other. Quilt the spaces between the waves with looping lines, each going in the direction in which the tulle has (probably) sagged. Leave the fish untouched. Cut the edges straight. You can quilt additional wavy lines by hand and dispense with the looping pattern.

Binding

(Lesson 13)

Bind the quilt edge with a medium-blue bias binding.

TIP

Do not iron over the tulle, since it melts easily!

Pin the fish to the background fabric and spread the tulle on top. Pin it on. Sew wavy cross lines across while changing the sewing direction. Remove the pins through the tulle netting.

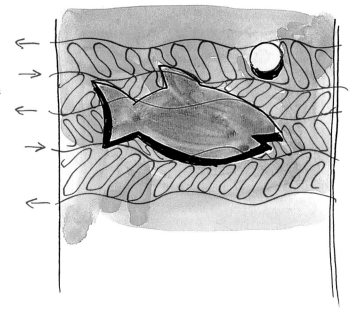

Assemble the quilt layers. Quilt looping lines between the waves, but leave the fish untouched.

Serenade
2¼ × 1⅝ yards (196 × 147 cm)

This "Serenade" quilt is an Italianate arabesque of colorful leaves that twine over a dark wool fabric. Instead of wool fabric you could also work with loden, a nonwoven fabric, or fine felt; it is important only that the edges of the fabric do not fray. The leaves are sewn on by hand in reverse applique technique.

■ Materials
Fabric
- 2¼ yards (2.00 m) dark, tightly woven wool fabric 1⅔ yards (150 cm) wide for the background.
- Sample book fabrics, solid, for about 290 leaves, at least 4" × 4" (10 × 10 cm); leave out very dark colors.

Or optionally use for the leaves:
- 3⅓ yards (3.00 m) rainbow fabric for about 290 squares of about 4" × 4" (10 × 10 cm).
- Ombre fabric, of all possible colors, total amount at least 3⅓ yards (3.00 m); leave out very dark shades.

Other
- Bright color crayon.
- Red sewing thread.
- If needed, cardboard for a stencil.
- Dark hand-quilting thread.
- 2½ × 1⅞ yards (220 × 170 cm) backing fabric.
- 2½ × 1⅞ yards (220 × 170 cm) volume fleece.
- Dark-blue quilting thread.
- 7⅔ yards (700 cm) wide black-satin bias binding for the binding.

■ Instructions
Drawing the Arabesque Design
Spread the wool fabric on a large surface, or fasten it to your design wall. Draw the arabesque design on the fabric with chalk, using a generous swing. To mark the lines, sew them with red thread using an about ⅓"-long (1 cm) running stitch.

Sewing the Leaves on by Hand
Cut your colored fabrics into squares of about 4" × 4" (10 × 10 cm) and lay them out ready. If possible, maintain the color sequence. Pin about twenty of these squares on either side of the central red line to maintain the color sequence. Now work on each leaf individually.

Spread out the wool fabric and trace the arabesque design. Rework the lines in a running stitch using red thread. Pin on a group of colored squares (4" × 4" [10 × 10 cm]) to the right and left of the marked line.

Take off the first square. At this place, cut out a pointed oval leaf shape from the wool fabric. The leaf should be about 1–1¼" (2.5–3 cm) wide and 2–2⅓" (5–6 cm) long. Cut freehand by eye, or make a leaf-shaped stencil from cardboard and use it for tracing. Use pins to fasten the four corners of the colored square behind the leaf-shaped opening. Use dark quilting thread and a fine running stitch to sew around the leaf shape at intervals of about 5 mm. Once the leaf is sewn on, trim back any protruding colored fabric on the wrong side of the piece of work, up to ⅓" (1 cm) from the seam.

Sew the leaves on, working leaf by leaf. Pin on the next set of squares along the twig and applique the leaves on as described. Take care that you get a balanced color distribution and make smooth transitions from one color to another. Remove the red marking stitches upon completion.

Quilting
(Lessons 11 and 12)
Quilt the center lines by hand and quilt once around each leaf, as well as around the scattered individual leaves on the open areas.

With a longarm quilting machine, first quilt the center line and once around each leaf. Then quilt an echo line along the leaf arabesque design, then a border of scrollwork, and again an echo line along the scrollwork border. Fill in the intervening spaces with a grid pattern.

Binding
(Lesson 13)
Bind the quilt with a wide black-satin bias.

Remove a square temporarily and cut out a leaf-shaped hole in the wool fabric.

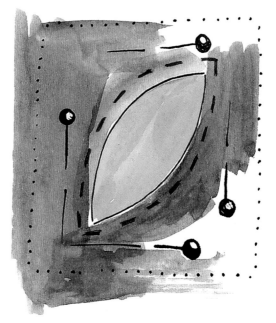

Pin the squares behind the opening and sew them to the edge using a running stitch at ¼" (5 mm) intervals (red dashed line).

From the wrong side, cut the colored fabric back to ⅓" (1 cm) from the seam (dotted line).

Quilting suggestion.

Colored Saucers
2 × 1¾ yards (180 × 155 cm)

The light background supports and emphasizes the round "colored saucers," whether they are kept in muted colors (like here), or are made in bright rainbow colors—you just can't go wrong.

■ Materials
Fabric
- Fabric sample book with fifty colors, 4" × 11" (10 × 28 cm) in size, to make each time two whole and one to two quarter circles.
- 2¾ yards (2.50 m) muslin (1⅔ yards [150 cm] wide), natural white, for the background.
- 5½ yards (5.00 m) white (1⅔ yards [150 cm] wide or bed linen) for the reverse applique and backing.

Or alternatively for the points:
- Six different ombre fabrics, all colors, ⅓ yard (0.30 m) each
- Fabric pack, thirty-five colors, 7¾" × 7¾" (20 × 20 cm), for four each of similar circles.
- Two yards (1.80 m) rainbow fabric.

Other
- 6" × 6" (15 × 15 cm) stiff cardboard for a stencil for the "window" openings.
- Compass or juice glass (30¾" [78 cm] diameter).
- Hard pencil or marker.
- 1⅓ yards (1.20 m) volume fleece (1⅔ yards [150 cm) wide) or plenty of volume fleece remnants, at least 4¾" × 4¾" (12 × 12 cm) in size.

■ Instructions
Making the Window Opening Stencil
Draw two diagonals from corner to corner on a piece of 6" × 6" (15 × 15 cm) cardboard to find the center point. Choose a juice glass with the same diameter (here 2¾" [7 cm]) or set a compass to a 1⅜" (3.5 cm) radius. Draw a circle on the cardboard. Cut out the circle.

Simple square (about 4" × 4" [10 × 10 cm]).

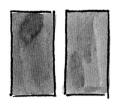

Two-color rectangles (4" × 2⅓" [10 × 6 cm]) to piece together into a square.

Four small squares (2⅓" × 2⅓" [6 × 6 cm]) to piece together into a larger square.

TIP
If you are using fabrics from a sample book, adjust the size of the circle according to the size of the pieces of fabric. The fabric piece must be at least ⅓" (1 cm) larger than the circle all around. Example: at least 4" × 4" (10 × 10 cm) of fabric for a circle diameter of 3¼" (8 cm).

Cutting Out
(Lesson 1: Basic Shapes)
For the front side, cut out 143 squares from the muslin and 286 squares from the white cotton fabric, each 6¾" × 6¾" (17 × 17 cm). The white squares are for the reverse applique, and the backing is for the various blocks. Cut the rainbow fabric into squares of about 4" × 4" (10 × 10 cm) and use the narrower and smaller remnants to make half and quarter colored squares. You need a total of 143 colored squares.

143 Colored Saucers
(Lesson 7: Reverse Applique Technique)
Place a white square on a muslin square and use a window stencil to draw a circle in the center. Sew all around on the line. Cut out the inside of the circle through both layers of fabric up to seam allowance width and notch the seam allowances close to the seam. Slide the white reverse applique fabric through the opening toward the back, then smooth down the edge. Iron now (!), because this is your only opportunity.

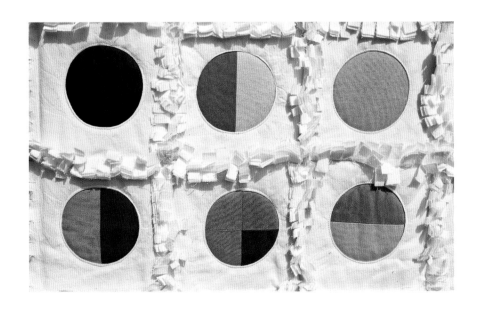

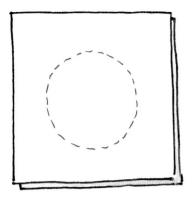

Place a white square (6¾" × 6¾" [17 × 17 cm]) on an equal-size muslin square, right sides facing. Draw a circle and sew all around on the line.

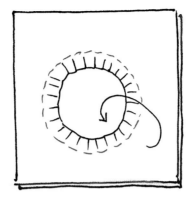

Cut out both layers of fabric inside the circle. Notch the seam allowance and pull the reverse applique fabric through the opening to the back.

Place a colored square (4" × 4" [10 × 10 cm]) behind the opening. Fasten to the front with four pins.

Pin a colored square approximately 4" × 4" (10 × 10 cm) behind each circle with four pins. You must insert the pins from the right side, near the circular opening. Now trim off the colored fabric on the wrong side to about ⅓" (1 cm) from the opening so it does not show through the top of the finished quilt. If you forget this step, later on, you will have to laboriously cut out the colored fabric protruding between the layers.

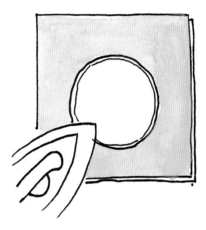

Iron the opening. This is your only opportunity to do this.

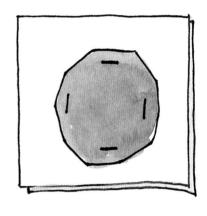

Trim back the colored fabric on the wrong side.

Finishing the Blocks

Cut out 143 squares of 4¾" × 4¾" (12 × 12 cm) from the volume fleece. Place a 6¾" × 6¾" (17 × 17 cm) square of backing on the table and place a fleece square on it. Lay the prepared circle block on top. Pin this "sandwich" together at all four corners. Use natural-color thread to quilt close to the edge around the circle. This fastens the layers together. You can now remove all the pins. If the layers have shifted slightly, trim back the protruding edges of the white fabric to the size of the muslin square.

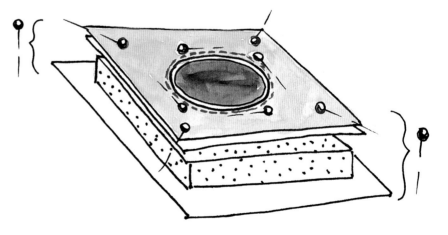

Preparing a sandwich: White backing fabric underneath (6¾" × 6¾" [17 × 17 cm]), volume fleece in the middle (4¾" × 4¾" [12 × 12 cm]), and the prepared circle unit on top. Pin all the layers, one atop the other, at the corners. Stitch along the edge of the circle, close to the edge.

Piecing the Quilt Together
(Lesson 9)

Arrange the blocks in thirteen horizontal rows of ten blocks each. Place the bright colors in the middle and the darker ones toward the outer edge, or find another arrangement that you like.

Since this is a rag quilt, the seam allowances must lie on the top layer and be stitched down extra wide. Sew the blocks together, placing them wrong sides facing and sew the seams ¾" (2 cm) deep.

TIP

To make it easier to keep to the 3/4" (2 cm) seam allowance width, attach a ¾"-wide (2 cm) marker out of tape to the right of the sewing machine needle, or attach a flat, long block to the needle plate.

Sew across the seam allowance of the lengthwise row; for the crosswise rows, you "skip over" the upright seam allowances from the preceding work step. Lockstitch the seam before and after the seam allowance. Stitch

around the outer edges, likewise at a ¾" (2 cm) distance. If you want, you can use a decorative stitch here.

Finishing

Use scissors to snip into the six layers of fabric at intervals of about ¼" (0.5 cm), close to the seam. Also snip into the sewn-around outer edges. Brush the edges with a stiff brush or put the quilt in the dryer so that the edges fray and become bushy.

Binding

No binding is attached to this quilt.

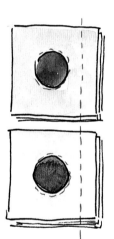

Lengthwise seams: Lay the blocks with wrong sides facing and sew with a ¾"-wide (2 cm) seam allowance. Do not cut the threads between the units.

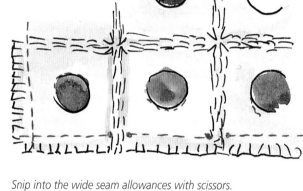

Snip into the wide seam allowances with scissors.

Crosswise seams: Lay the rows with wrong sides facing and skip over the "standing up" seam allowances of the lengthwise seams. Lockstitch the thread before and after each seam allowance. Also sew around the outside edges.

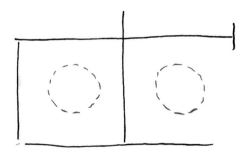

View of the wrong side.

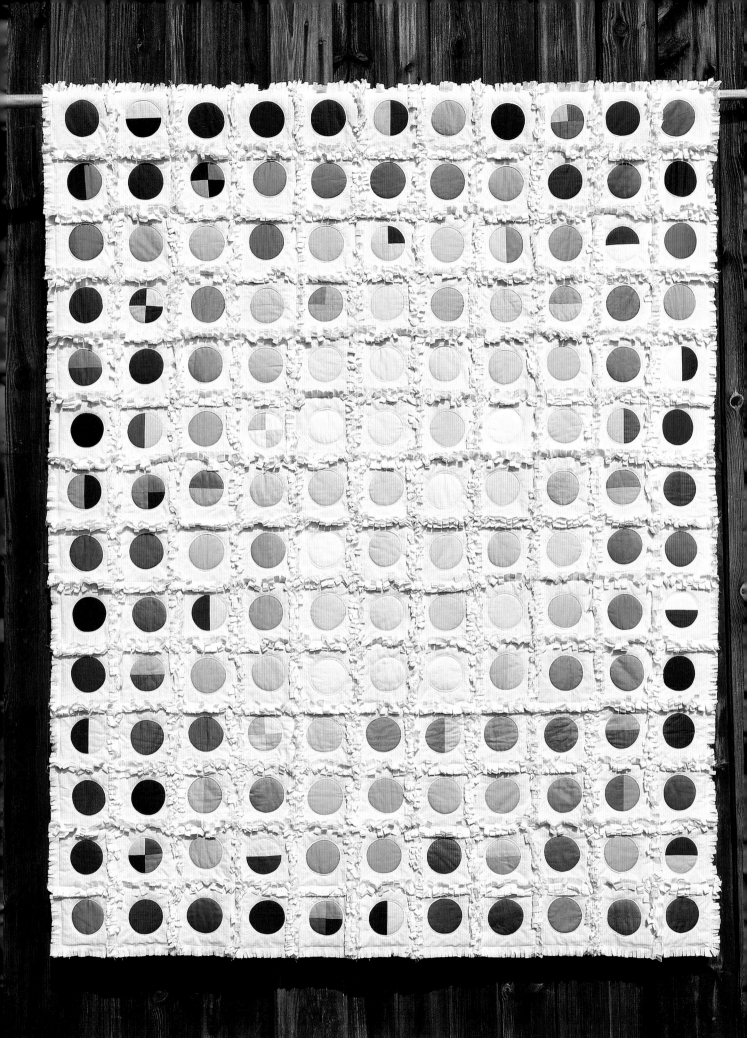

Lesson 9:
Piecing the Quilt Together Efficiently

Place the blocks of your quilt on your work surface or floor in an arrangement that you like.

In your head, number the lengthwise rows 1, 2, 3, etc. Mark each of the top blocks with a pin.

Place the blocks of row 2, right sides facing, on top of the blocks of row 1.

Stack the assembled blocks, offset slightly, one atop the other. Start with the lower pairs of blocks. Lay the row to the left of your sewing machine. Keeping a short distance between the work and sewing machine helps to prevent the blocks from twisting.

Start with the top uppermost block pair. Sew exactly along the right edge of the block pair at presser foot width. *Do not* cut away the threads between the blocks (= chain piecing).

Now sew the crosswise seams of the block chain. Start with the two lowest pairs. Lay the first pair, right sides facing, on the next one and sew the edges together at presser foot width. At the seam crossing, press one seam allowance upward and the other downward.

Continue in this manner, and make sure that the finished sewn part of the double row is always at the top, and the next pair to be sewn on is beneath. This lets you keep the seam allowances in view and know in which direction the following seam allowance needs to be pressed.

Finish the double row and iron all seam allowances for the crosswise seams downward. The pin you inserted at the beginning helps you find the "top" of the rows.

Sew more double rows from rows 3 and 4, 5, and 6, etc.

Iron all the seam allowances for the crosswise seams of the second double row upward, all those of the third row downward again, etc.

If your quilt is composed of an odd number of rows, work the last three as follows: Assemble the second-to-last two rows as described, and then, before you sew the lengthwise seams, attach the blocks of the last row. Do not cut off the threads between the blocks. In this case the crosswise seams reach over the width of three blocks.

When all the double rows are finished then attach these. The seam allowances, which you have ironed around, now always lie in opposite directions; this creates flat seam intersections.

Finally, iron the quilt top first on the wrong side and then on the right side.

Advantages
This systematic, offset stacking method allows you to design the quilt top in a different room from the room where you have your sewing machine. Transport the stacked rows of blocks on a long quilting yardstick, like you would on a tray.

This systematic way of folding and stacking reduces the risk of twisting one of the blocks to a minimum.

Chain piecing, where you do not cut off the threads between the blocks, prevents the blocks from twisting.

If you lay the stacked blocks to the left of the sewing machine, you have the shortest "path" to the needle. This also helps prevent twisting.

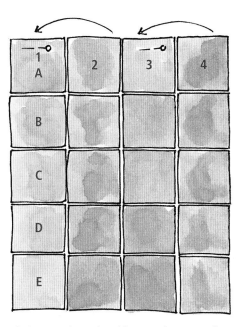

Piecing together pairs with crosswise seams. Start with the bottom pair.

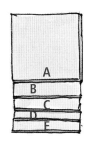

Lay the blocks of each right row, right sides facing, over the left row.

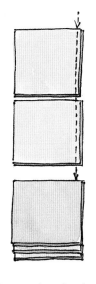

Stagger the pairs of blocks. Start from below. The top pair is uppermost.

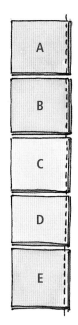

Sew the block pairs together along the right edge.

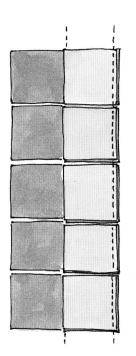

Do not cut the threads between the units.

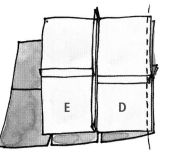

Solution for the last three rows of an odd number of rows.

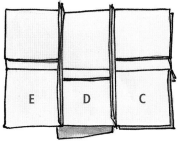

The sewn pairs always lie on top. Press the seam allowances in opposite directions.

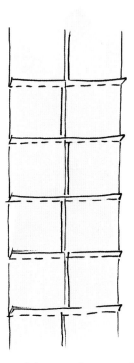

Iron all the crosswise seams of the first double row downward and those of the next double row upward; the next downward again, etc.

Lesson 10:
Borders

Measuring the Quilt

Basically, you should measure your quilt crosswise and lengthwise through the center of the finished, ironed quilt top—never along the edge. The length of the border strips is based on these measurements. To be sure, measure the quilt top again after sewing on each border strip.

Borders with Straight Corners

If necessary, straighten the edges of the quilt or pillow top. Decide on a suitable strip width and cut the border strips. Piece together several strips until you reach the required length. First sew the border strips to the two long sides of the quilt. The strips for the top and bottom edges are sewn on

last. You figure out the length of the strips for the upper and lower edges from the measurement of the quilt edge plus the sewn-on strips. For this, measure for the quilt again across the middle.

Borders with Cornerstones

Cornerstones are square, and are generally the same size as the edge strip is wide. Cut the border strips exactly as long as the measurement to the quilt edge. Put a cornerstone on both ends of the strips for the upper and lower edges. Iron the seam allowances to the strips. First sew the strips onto the long sides of the quilt, and iron the seam allowances outward. Then sew the two strips with the attached cornerstones to the top and bottom edges of the quilt.

Lesson 11:
Assembling the Quilt

Iron the sewn quilt top carefully. Prepare a quilt backing that is about 4" (10 cm) larger on all sides than the quilt top is. The fleece must be just as big.

Spread the backing fabric right side down on a large work surface and secure the corners with tape. Lay the layer of fleece on top and smooth it out.

Lay the quilt top, with the right side up, on top of this and smooth it out, working from the center to the edges.

Baste across the quilt top at hand-width intervals. Stick the long basting needle through to the table surface or to the floor, then turn the needle point upward without putting your hand under the quilt. This prevents making creases and shifting the layers. If possible, work from the middle of the quilt top outward, or start along an outer edge. Continue basting, row by row, up to the opposite edge. At the same time, you can smooth any creases toward the still-open edge.

Now quilt the project by hand or by machine.

Lesson 12:
Quilting with a Sewing Machine

Machine Quilting
Use the fabric mover on your machine. Sew along the predrawn straight lines (such as for grid quilting) or in the seam shadow. Use upper and lower thread of the same color, in case the lower thread shows on the top.

Outline Quilting: The quilt line winds around in a pattern, either in the seam shadow or at a seam allowance width distance. You do not need to presketch anything.

Grid Quilting: A regular grid of straight lines criss-crosses the quilt top lengthwise and crosswise or diagonally. Presketch the lines.

Freehand Machine Quilting
Insert the darning foot of your sewing machine (very rarely you can do freehand quilting without any foot at all). Lower the fabric mover and/or adjust the pressure of the needle bar to 0. Use the same thread for the upper and lower thread and if necessary, loosen the needle thread tension a little. Set the stitching straight. The stitch length setting does not matter. The three layers of the quilt are basted together or glued together with removable spray adhesive. Practice first on a sample piece.

Lower the presser foot (this is important because of the thread tension). For some machine types, the foot should be half lowered. Now press down the foot pedal steadily, and using both hands lying to the right and left of the needle, guide the quilt through under the sewing machine.

> **TIP**
> To be able to guide the quilt evenly under the machine, gardening gloves with rubber nubs or with latex coating prove to be a useful aid.

Work at a relatively quick sewing speed. With practice, the stitches will be of the same length, and your motions will be even. Lockstitch the threads at the beginning and end of the quilting line with a few stitches on the spot, or draw it to the back of the quilt and knot it there.

Stippling and Other Top Patterns: Stippling means quilting a curved line in a meandering pattern densely on the quilt top, without letting it cross over itself. Invent more top patterns: intertwined circles, flames, grasses, water lines, arcs, vines, flowers, or leaves. Work in a continuous line and interrupt the work as little as possible.

Motif Quilting: Trace a quilt pattern with lines that extend without interruption. Quilt along the drawn lines. With practice, you can quilt beautiful motifs without tracing them on beforehand.

Quilting with a Sewing Machine

Lesson 13: Binding

The "binding" is the outermost strips of fabric that encloses the quilt edge. It is sewn on when the quilted piece is finished.

Preparing the Quilt

To straighten a quilt edge, use a marker to draw a straight line along all of the edges. Use a long ruler when doing this. For a 90 degree corner, place a larger object with rectangular corners (such as cardboard, a picture frame, etc.) on it, or orient it to the corner of your work table; for smaller pieces use a cutting-mat grid. Baste along the drawn lines around the entire quilt and then trim back all the protruding fabric and fleece that is 1 mm outside this line. Now the quilt is ready for binding.

> **TIP**
> An aluminum rail from a hardware store works well as a long ruler.

Straight-Cut, Double-Folded Binding

Cut the fabric strips for a straight binding 2⅓" (6 cm) wide, unless otherwise specified. Piece as many strips together as needed until you reach the length of the quilt circumference.

Iron the binding strip lengthwise, wrong sides facing in the middle. Lay the strip along the quilt edge, with the open edge facing outward, and stitch along it at presser foot width.

Cut off the protruding strips at the end of the first quilt edge. Fold the closed edge of the strip toward the back of the quilt and pin it there firmly. Then sew the next strip onto the next edge; at the start leave about ¾" (2 cm) of overlap so you can fold a neat corner. Work through the first three strips in this way. When sewing on the fourth strip, leave an additional ¾" (2 cm) of overlap at the bottom corner. Carefully fold the strips toward the quilt back on all the edges and pin and hem it firmly there by hand, right above the sewing line.

Make the corners by folding back the open, short edge of the strip up to the quilt edge and then folding the strips toward the back of the quilt. Sew to the short open section of the bias strip to the corner.

Sewing on straight cut, lengthwise folded strips.

Fold the strips backward and pin them firmly.

Let the beginning of the next strip overlap somewhat.

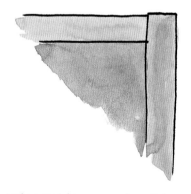

Make a straight corner and sew it down.

Binding with Ready-Made Bias Binding

Buy bias binding of a matching color, ready folded, enough for the length of the total circumference of the quilt plus a 7¾" (20 cm) safety margin. Lay the bias binding on the quilt right side down and unfold the right edge. Sew the strip to the quilt edge along the ironed fold. At the start of the following strip, leave an overlap of ¾" (2 cm) each time, and do likewise at the end of the last strip (as described above). Fold the bias binding to the back of the quilt and hem it directly to the edge of the seam by hand. Make straight corners.

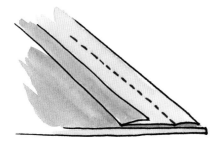

Unfold the right edge of the bias binding. Sew into the seam on the quilt edge.

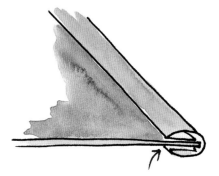

Fold the bias binding to the back and hem on.

Lesson 14:
Cushion with Zipper Closing

Cut the cushion backing fabric so that it is as wide as the cushion top and 4" (10 cm) longer.

Place the backing fabric lengthwise along the sewing mat. Spread out the section in the lower third crosswise. Place these cut edges right sides facing and mark both the beginning and end of the zipper with a pin each.

Sew 2" (5 cm) inside the edge in this order:

1. From the upper edge to the upper zipper marker, with normal stitch length;
2. Make some back stitches at the marker;
3. up to the lower marker with the longest stitch length (basting stitch);
4. Make some back stitches at the lower marker;
5. to the bottom edge with normal stitch length.

Unfold the seam and iron it. Fold down both edges up to the seam and iron over it once again. Alternatively, you can also cast over the two edges with a zigzag stitch.

Open up the seam at the beginning of the loosely stitched section to about 2" (5 cm) wide and push the zipper slider from behind through the opening toward the front side. Pin the zipper firmly with extra-long pins to the wrong side of the fabric along the loosely stitched seam.

Work in this order at a presser foot width on the right side of the fabric:

1. Begin at the starting point (arrow);
2. open the zipper 2" (5 cm) wide;
3. sew up to the zipper slider;
4. raise the presser foot and close the zipper;
5. sew farther up to the bottom end of the zipper;
6. sew a bar across the zipper at the bottom (tapered or straight).
7. turn the cushion backing in the new sewing direction;
8. sew along on the other side of the zipper up to the slider;
9. raise the presser foot and open the zipper;
10. sew the seam to the end;
11. and again sew a bar at the top.

Remove the pins and remove the loosely stitched seam section using a seam ripper. Pull the thread remnants from the fabric edges.

Finishing the Cushion

When hand quilting a cushion top, make sure that you do not quilt beyond the measurement of 19½" × 19½" (50 × 50 cm) so that you do not snip the quilting thread when trimming the cushion top. Trim the finished quilted cushion top to exactly 20½" × 20½" (52 × 52 cm).

If you have machine quilted the cushion top, then trim it now to 20½" × 20½" (52 × 52 cm). Severing the quilting lines does no harm, because the edges disappear into the outseam of the cushion.

Open the zipper about 4" (10 cm) wide. Lay the cushion backing, with the attached zipper, right side up on your work surface and spread the 20½" ×

20½" (52 × 52 cm) cushion top, right side down, atop it. Make sure that the motif of the cushion top is not upside down.

Pin together the cushion top and backing firmly with pins, right sides facing, and stitch at presser foot width around the cushion. Only now should you trim back the cushion backing to the edge of the cushion top. Cast over all the edges with a zigzag stitch.

Turn out the cushion top through the zipper opening and insert a cushion.

TIP
You can achieve beautifully crafted corners with the following technique. Use your forefinger to grasp the cushion in the corner. With your other hand, fold the corner seam allowance horizontally inward, then the adjacent seam allowance vertically over it. Press your thumbs on it and hold the corner firmly between your thumb and forefinger. Turn out the corner without loosening your grip. After turning the corner will remain there, and it is not necessary to cut off the seam allowance.

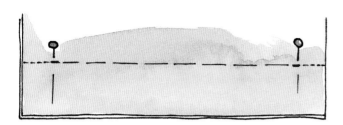

Prepare the seam for the zipper. Sew between the pin markers with very long stitches.

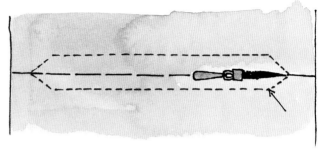

Pin the zipper firmly with long pins from the wrong side. Put the zipper slider through a section of the separated seam.

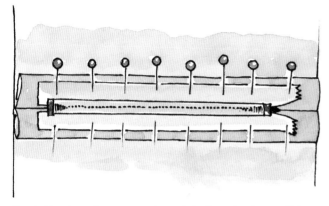

Sew in the zipper (arrow = starting point). Open the zipper a little or close it completely as necessary.

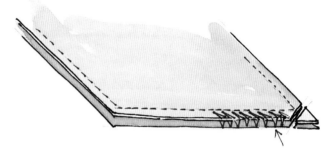

Lay the cushion pieces one atop the other and sew along the outer edge of the cushion. Trim back the edges of the cushion and cast over the outer edge with a zigzag stitch.

Cushion with Zipper Closing

Imprint design and realization: Bernadette Mayr
Editing: Claudia Wollny
Editor: Angelika Klein
Photography: Sabine Münch
Styling: Gundula Manson
Technical drawings: Bernadette Mayr

Thanks

I thank my sister Irmgard for the division of labor and her support in sewing the quilts; my girlfriend Gundula for the endless number of "small" pieces of work, such as turning reverse applique openings and cutting denim into squares, as well as testing for comprehensibility and proofreading the instructions; Claudia Wollny for careful editing; Claudia Pfeil for inspiring courses in longarm quilting; and Sabine Münch from Berlin for the stunning photos.

Irmgard Stängl/Bernadette Mayr